Praise for E

"New knowledge from ancient wisdom! Claudia Dillaire brings the proven magic of the ancient Egyptians to bear on the financial trials and tribulations of modern times. With clear and precise instructions, she opens the door to the past and thereby brings the light of hope to the future. A fascinating and decidedly utilitarian work that is a joy to read."

—*Raymond Buckland, bestselling author of* Buckland's Book of Spirit Communications

"Coming at a time when this type of magic is needed more than ever, this book is a brilliant introduction to ancient Egyptian deities. It reveals the magic of the common folk, not just that of a priesthood isolated within its temples. Dillaire makes this modern adaptation of the ancient techniques and concepts practical for Wiccans, Pagans, and those interested in following the spiritual path of a culture that was ancient before Greece and Rome began. Highly recommended."

—*Donald Michael Kraig,*
bestselling author of Modern Magick

"Straightforward and focused, this compendium is complete in itself, each spell specifically set forth and described from start to finish. The book includes correspondences and historically accurate references, which will delight the lovers of all things Egyptian and those who crave a historical basis to their spellwork. This book should sit on the shelves of all practical magical workers and spell crafters."

—*Dana D. Eilers, author of* The Practical Pagan

"An eminently useful and much-needed resource for those who are students and practitioners of herbal magic. Not only does Dillaire offer the reader much information about the integration of ancient Egyptian magic and wisdom into modern herbal work, but she introduces the pantheon of one of the primary sources of the western magical tradition. Well-organized and thoughtful, this book has the ability to change the course of one's life."

—*Rev. Paul Beyerl, Wiccan priest,*
instructor in herbalism studies,
and author of The Master Book of Herbalism

EGYPTIAN
PROSPERITY MAGIC

About the Author

Claudia R. Dillaire is the author of three books on Egyptian magic. She has been a solitary practitioner for thirteen years. Though she is a researcher of ancient civilizations and mythology, her primary expertise is ancient Egypt. When she is not researching, she works as a freelance copyeditor and proofreader, as well as writing mystery novels set in late New Kingdom Egypt. Her other books include *Egyptian Love Spells and Rituals* and *Egyptian Revenge Spells*. She maintains a website for her freelance work and writing (www .ewitchfreelancing.com) and a blog for writers (claudiardillaire .blogspot.com), in addition to a presence on Facebook. She lives in Arizona.

CLAUDIA R. DILLAIRE

EGYPTIAN
PROSPERITY MAGIC

Spells & Recipes For Financial Empowerment

Llewellyn Publications
Woodbury, Minnesota

First Edition
Third Printing, 2019

Cover art ©2011 GUIZIOU Franck/Hemis/photolibrary. All rights reserved.
Cover design by Adrienne W. Zimiga
Interior art © Llewellyn art department
Llewellyn is a registered trademark of Llewellyn Worldwide Ltd.

Library of Congress Cataloging-in-Publication Data
Dillaire, Claudia R.
   Egyptian prosperity magic : spells & recipes for financial empowerment.
— 1st ed.
      p. cm.
   Includes bibliographical references (p.   ) and index.
   ISBN 978-0-7387-2677-9
1. Finance, Personal--Miscellanea. 2. Magic, Egyptian. I. Title.
   BF1623.F55D55 2011
   133.4'4—dc23

                                          2011017035

Llewellyn Worldwide does not participate in, endorse, or have any authority or responsibility concerning private business transactions between our authors and the public.

All mail addressed to the author is forwarded but the publisher cannot, unless specifically instructed by the author, give out an address or phone number.

Any Internet references contained in this work are current at publication time, but the publisher cannot guarantee that a specific location will continue to be maintained. Please refer to the publisher's website for links to authors' websites and other sources.

Llewellyn Publications
A Division of Llewellyn Worldwide Ltd.
2143 Wooddale Drive
Woodbury, Minnesota 55125-2989
www.llewellyn.com

Printed in the United States of America

CONTENTS

ACKNOWLEDGMENTS

With all books, it takes a collaborative effort to produce one; I create the words and content, but others edit, critique, and assist in a variety of ways. This is where I get to thank them for their time and generosity in bringing my words to life.

To William J. Dykens, my partner in life, for always being there and for being so patient and understanding when I write late into the night.

To Russell and Janice Smith; Russ for testing some of the oils, and Janice, for allowing me to use her husband, again, as my guinea pig.

To Abigail Richon and Doug Wilcox, for being my own personal computer techs; when technology fails me, you two never do.

To Adam Schaab, acquisitions editor at Llewellyn, for seeing that "something" in my writing; thank you for giving me the opportunity to bring more Egyptian magic to the public. And to all the people behind the scenes at Llewellyn, who made this book the best it could be.

INTRODUCTION

Egyptian magic has often been overlooked or only mentioned in passing in Paganism. And yet, the ancient Egyptians left a wealth of written materials on papyri, tomb walls, obelisks, and temples. So who better to learn from on the subject of prosperity than a civilization that survived for at least five thousand years?

Granted, prosperity in 2011 BCE was quite different from prosperity in 2011 CE, but some things remain constant. Home and hearth, food and clothing, health and happiness, family and friends are the same concerns now as then. The ancient civilizations had an advantage, however, for they had magic, and the gods, on their side.

My aim in writing this book is to shed some light on the magical practices of the ancient Egyptians. However, my book, though based on many of their recorded spells, is not meant as an historical treatise. I write about what I am passionate about—Egyptian magic—and how I practice that magic. And in so doing, I hope to bridge the gap between the ancient and the modern. I want to offer an alternative to Wicca, or for these practices to be used complementarily to Wicca. My first book, *Egyptian Love Spells and Rituals*, blended Wicca with Egyptian magic, but Egyptian magic is fulfilling enough to stand alone. My second book, *Egyptian Revenge Spells*, dealt with the concepts of curses, protection, and revenge from the Egyptian perspective.

Many assumptions have been made concerning how magic was practiced by ancient cultures, and without clear-cut instructions, what we "know" is still mostly assumption. Can we really be sure the Druids constructed Stonehenge and what its purpose was? Do we really know how and why deities were worshipped by the Babylonians, Assyrians, or Minoans? Some evidence is clear—temples, tomb paintings—but without written documentation, we can only speculate.

The Egyptians left records behind, but this may also not be definitive. Some papyri in museums today are thought to be copies of older documents, some papyri lack key pieces of the puzzle, and some carvings were used as propaganda for the masses.

What we do know is this: the Egyptians loved their country and their gods, and the Egyptian priests and/or kings were solely responsible for appeasing those deities. The practice of Egyptian magic today casts you, the practitioner, as the high priest or priestess. *You* are the connection to the deities, *you* make the offerings, and *you* reap the rewards. *You* can increase your prosperity, starting today.

Each and every day we are confronted with financial stresses and economic woes: housing meltdown and foreclosures; layoffs and outsourcing; rising food and gas prices; and stock market fluctuation—can it get any worse? I am not an economist or a financial expert; far from it. I struggle to make ends meet just like you do, and I cannot predict what the future holds. Hopefully we have seen the worst of the recent economic crisis, but maybe a little magic can help preserve what assets you already have, as well as bringing more prosperity to you.

ONE

Prosperity, the Egyptians, and Magic

In the agrarian society of ancient Egypt, magic and prosperity interacted somewhat differently than they do in our society today. A good harvest, the births of strong cattle, sheep, and sons, and the annual inundation of the Nile were necessary for prosperity in ancient Egypt. However, it was not individual prosperity that was important to the Egyptians, for if the country flourished, all its inhabitants reaped the benefits. In times of hardship, the king was considered directly responsible as the representative of the gods on earth. If the gods were not worshipped, if offerings were not made, the gods could withhold the sustenance provided by the Nile. All prospered or suffered, regardless of social status.

Needless to say, my requests of and offerings to the gods are not the same as they might have been millennia ago. I do offer wine and beer to the gods, but sacks of grain and incense would put a strain on anyone's budget. My petitions are not for abundant crops and a healthy herd, but for finding a publisher, a job closer to home, or enough money to pay the mortgage. Times change and worship should evolve as well; I don't think many Christians pray for protection against the plague, although it was probably a popular petition to God in the Dark Ages. I'm sure the ancients would be quite amused by how we make our livings and how much we worry over our careers and money. For what defines success in our culture, such as owning a home, a brand-new car, and electronic gadgets for every use—not to mention the stress that comes from maintaining the pace necessary to keep up—would be as foreign to an ancient Egyptian as his world would be to us. We equate money, possessions, and social status with prosperity and, in many cases, will go to any lengths to achieve or attain what we desire.

The ancient Egyptians did not have a monetary system until late in their civilization, specifically the Greek and Roman periods. The Egyptians relied on the barter system to obtain goods and services, as gold did not have the same importance it does today. One ancient chronicler reported that gold was as plentiful as grains of sand in the desert, which was likely an exaggeration. However, trees and the resins they provided were very important in an arid desert country like Egypt. Note that two of the three gifts brought by the wise men to the Christ child were the resins frankincense and myrrh, thus attesting to the value they commanded.

To gain favor or to appease the gods, offerings were made of the first crops harvested and words were spoken in hopes of continued prosperity. If the offerings and words led to bountiful harvests, the words would be used again in subsequent rituals. If the harvest was not plentiful, different offerings and words would be used, hoping to appease the gods. Eventually, the words, as spells, would be written on papyrus so they could be spoken again and again to ensure prosperity.

The most common techniques used in prosperity magic are the same as the ones employed for other types of magic in ancient Egypt. Offerings, swallowing an enchanted liquid, and letters to the dead are the methods we will explore and use in this book.

Offerings (Sacrifices): Naturally, the most common technique would be an offering of some sort to the gods.

Beer and wine, bread, sheaves of grain from the first harvest, and in some cases, the ritual slaughter of cattle, sheep, and other animals would be offered to the gods in ancient Egypt.

Swallowing: Ingesting enchanted liquids or dissolving ink was a common practice to release the magic in a spell. Most Egyptians were illiterate and would be unable to read a spell. So the spell would be written upon a piece of papyrus by the priest, the requestor would take it home, soak it in water, beer, or wine, and when the ink had dissolved, the liquid would be drunk to release the magic. The act of swallowing would allow the requestor to "acquire" the power of the written word. Magical swallowing survived even beyond the rule of the Greeks and Romans, though I do not recommend swallowing dissolved ink, unless the ink is made from grape, pomegranate, or another fruit. See appendix A for some harmless substances that may be used to create magical ink.

Letters to the Dead: Petitions would be inscribed on whatever was available—pottery shards, clay tablets, or papyrus—and left at the tomb of deceased relatives. The dead were petitioned because it was felt they could assist the living in magical ways. In some cases, a dead person or persons would be perceived as being the root of a problem, and petitioning them in this way would appease them.

I am often asked why my spells and rituals have a Wiccan feel to them. The answer may lie in the fact that the practices of the Egyptians have been borrowed and expanded upon by many other cultures and religions. The use of incense, lighting of candles, and making of offerings, all with roots in ancient Egyptian magical practices, have been incorporated into Catholicism, for example, but that certainly does not mean that Catholicism is a form of Egyptian magic, or Wicca, or Paganism. *Practices* can be similar but *beliefs* determine the path one follows. Could it be that Wicca has drawn upon Egyptian practices, which is why they seem so familiar?

Magic permeated all aspects of Egyptian life, from the shaking of rattles to chase away evil spirits at birth to the extensive—not to mention expensive and time consuming—mummification rituals at death. And though written records exist for many of their practices, we may wonder how the average Egyptian worshipped his deities. The answer, quite simply, is by doing practically nothing.

Originally it was the king (or *per-aa*, from which we get the term *pharaoh*) who handled the important temple tasks, being the living intermediary with the gods.

But with so many gods, so large a country, and so many temples, it became impossible for the king to attend to each and every god on a daily basis. He appointed priests to handle the duties associated with serving the temple gods. In so doing, the priesthood eventually became almost as powerful as the king, owning much of the land in Egypt by the era of the New Kingdom.

Management of the temple complexes fell to the First God's Servant. Each day, the god had to be awakened, removed from his shrine, bathed, dressed, and fed by the high priest of the temple. Incense was burned as an offering to the god at the appropriate times of the day; in the evening, the god would be disrobed and put back into the shrine until the following day. Lesser priests handled food and incense preparation, and, in some cases, dispensed herbal cures. The First God's Servant held a full-time position running a temple complex, but a lesser priest might only serve at the temple for three months at a time, the rest of his time spent in his normal occupation as a scribe, carpenter, or goldsmith. In other temples, the attendants to the god were priestesses who worked with the God's Wife, a title and political position of power enjoyed by the chief wife of the king, generally speaking, or his eldest daughter.

The priesthood eventually evolved into a powerful political force, with sons inheriting their position from father and grandfather, and was not seen as a religious calling. Although the priesthood was a business, and a very influential one, it was still imbued with magic, for magic was present in all things in ancient Egypt. Some priests took their duties quite seriously, while others, I'm sure, looked upon their occupation as a stepping-stone in social standing and status in the community.

The average Egyptian had a niche at home, used for ancestor worship and for veneration of the local and state gods. It might contain a votive statue of an ibis for the god Thoth or a cat votive for Hathor or Bast. The only time the average Egyptian was even allowed to look upon the statue of a god was during certain annual festivals. At some festivals, questions could even be posed to the god, through a priest, and the god statue would respond, through interpretations from the priest.

Magic and the gods were so important to the people of ancient Egypt that even the Greeks who ruled the country, Cleopatra included, took Egyptian names and worshipped the Egyptian gods. Cleopatra even went so far as to learn to speak Egyptian, endearing herself to the people. As a testament to the enduring nature of Egyptian culture, many Greeks and Romans held Egypt in high regard. It was *the* place to see in the ancient world.

So how can the average person today practice Egyptian magic? As I said earlier, Egyptian magic casts you, the practitioner, in the role of high priest or priestess. You determine your needs for prosperity, you make the offerings to the gods, and you reap the benefits. Let's look at the following example of how to use Egyptian magic to get a new or better job. But remember, using magic isn't going to make the job fall in your lap. Lighting a candle every evening and wishing for a new job is only a start, and more needs to be done—scan the want ads in the newspaper, post a résumé online, network with people you know.

Suppose that you find just the job you want in the newspaper and brush up that résumé, but you want to make sure yours is the one that catches the HR director's attention. So you construct a spell, including the newspaper ad or a copy of your résumé, and perform it a night or two before applying. You get the call back you were hoping for and learn that the job is everything you have always wanted. Think of that spell as a neon sign on your résumé, shouting your worth to the company and getting you noticed.

Maybe you are really stressing about the interview; this is your dream job and you know your life will be so much better if you get hired. A more intensive spell, done over a longer period of time, may be just right for you to let the gods know how much you really want this position. You construct the perfect spell, expressing from the heart your fears, needs, and desires regarding the job. The day of the interview arrives and, lo and behold, you are cool, calm, collected; you have all the confidence you could ever need. That spell helped give you the right attitude for the interview and the job is offered to you.

The preceding examples are obviously simplistic, but illustrate the varying degrees of effort you may have to expend to get what you want. The outcomes above were positive, but it could have worked in just the opposite fashion. For example, you search the papers for months, every résumé you send out seems to end up in the circular file, and even when you do finally get an interview, you know the position will never be offered to you. Is it the magic that failed, or is it your attitude? It could be one, the other, or both. In such a case, try a different spell, change your résumé, or consult with a recruiter to see if you are presenting the right image. Use every avenue imaginable, *including magic*, to reach your goals; a little magic can go a long way.

TWO

Spellcasting, Egyptian Style

Egyptian prosperity magic can be very simple and straightforward. The gods understood the need for prosperity, for without it, the priests would have no offerings. When approaching prosperity spellwork, I like to employ the following methods, previously discussed in chapter 1, which the gods would have understood, even in 2011 BCE.

The most common method would be an offering to the gods, but since most of us don't raise our own crops and animals, a gift of bread, fresh or dried herbs, or a simple goblet of wine or beer will do. The Egyptians drank a great deal of beer and would certainly not be offended by the gesture; they even had a goddess of beer,

Menqet. Placing offerings of business cards, résumés, legal documents, coins, paper money, or credit cards on your altar can help you to focus your attention, not to mention keep you from using the credit card while working the spell.

One word here about résumés. If you are submitting a paper version, you don't want it stained with oil; what I have found just as effective is to hold the résumé in your hands, high above your altar, and pass it through the incense smoke and over the candle flame. Try not to singe it, of course. You can also sprinkle it with herbs before sending; just make sure this does not stain the paper. To further complicate matters, with the advent of electronic media, we don't always have to type up a résumé—we can simply e-mail it. What is a magical practitioner to do? As with any magical tool, your computer can be anointed with oil, just not a lot of it. I have had great success by putting a drop of oil in my hands, rubbing them together, and just gently touching my laptop. The oil can be wiped right off, but the computer has been anointed for your purposes. Additionally, you can always sprinkle the magical herbs around the laptop while submitting a résumé online.

As I mentioned earlier, most ancient Egyptians were unable to read or write and would not have the expertise to perform a spell, so they often sought the help of their local priest. He would listen to the problem and might send them home with an appropriate spell written on papyrus. This would be soaked in wine, beer, or water until the ink dissolved, creating an enchanted liquid, which would then be drunk to infuse the person with the spell. I do not advocate drinking anything with ink in it, unless the ink is made from fruit juice. Rather than drink enchanted liquids, I prefer to use them to water houseplants, pour them around my property to protect it, or sprinkle in an office before a job interview. Be creative and find ways to get your magic where it needs to be to make the most impact.

Letters to the dead were used to lift a curse, to bring good fortune, or for any number of concerns; the ancient Egyptians felt that even if a person was dead, he or she could still have an effect on earthly matters. Petitions may still be written and kept on your altar to focus you during spellwork, or you can use a shortened version in the form of incantation papers. Write the incantation on slips of paper prior to beginning the spell and keep them on the altar. At the appropriate time in the spellwork, recite the words, light the paper from the candle flame, and drop it immediately into a cauldron or fireproof bowl. Burning the paper sends forth the wish, thus releasing the magic. You will find that all the spells in chapter four use incantation papers, but you may omit that step if you want, without fear that the spell won't work.

Though not really an Egyptian form of magical expression, I often employ the use of a spell bottle, which has been employed in the hoodoo tradition, among others, for a wide range of purposes. In medieval times, witch bottles were created to guard against witches by filling them with noxious liquids, foul herbs, and rusty nails or shards of glass. Similarly, spell bottles or spell jars can be filled with materials related to or symbolizing the issue at hand. Filling a jar with honey to sweeten a situation or lemon juice or vinegar to sour a relationship can be an effective way to express one's magical energy. Use whatever is handy, but if you want to place your spell bottle in the freezer, you might want to use a plastic bottle or container instead of glass.

A spell bottle of sorts can be a very effective method of debt control. Take all your credit cards (or all but one, reserved strictly for emergencies), put them in a container, fill it with water, and place it in the back of your freezer. Instead of buying that new pair of shoes on impulse, you'll have time to sit and think about it while your credit cards thaw out. You might find you really don't *need* those new shoes; you just *want* them. Additionally, candles may be burned atop a spell jar to seal it and to solidify the magic performed, just don't do this with plastic containers.

Spellcasting Basics

Any room of the house is appropriate for spellcasting. Choose an area away from traffic where you can have some time alone. When performing spells, this should be a time of complete concentration—do not allow distractions to interfere with your needs. Keep burning candles away from children and pets; once the candle is lit, it may be moved to a higher location if necessary to avoid any mishaps.

Tools

Each spell in this book is specifically designed for some type of prosperity magic. All the ingredients have been chosen carefully to maximize the effects of your spell. See the explanation before each spell for any additional items you may need to perform that particular one.

The following items are required for any spell in this book:

- A candleholder (and optional dish)
- An incense burner
- A plate or saucer

- A small bowl for mixing herbs
- A fireproof bowl or cauldron (if you choose to burn incantation papers)
- A paper towel or cloth rag
- Matches or a lighter
- A quartz crystal (raw or tumbled)
- Personal items

Most of these things are self-explanatory. I often put a dish under the candles to save on cleanup in case they drip or puddle. The incense burner should match the type you choose: loose, stick, or cone. If a burner is not available, you may use a dish of sand or dirt; place the cone on top, or stick the incense stick into it. There is no harm in improvising and it will not affect the outcome of the spell.

The plate or saucer will be used as an offering dish. The herbs and/or personal items will be placed upon it. It may be glass, ceramic, or plastic, whatever is available and small enough to fit on your altar or work area. The small bowl will be used to mix the herbs listed for each spell.

The bowl or cauldron will be used if you choose to burn incantation papers. Since paper can flash up quickly, it is advisable to light it and drop it into the bowl or cauldron. The intent of a spell is to bring prosperity, not to lose everything by burning your house down. If you wish to hold one end of an incantation paper with tweezers, again, that will not affect the outcome and may save you from burned fingers.

Since you will be anointing candles and rubbing the plate with a drop of oil, it is very important to have something to wipe your hands on. A paper towel may be discarded when the spellwork is complete, or you may wish to use a rag that can be laundered and used again in future spellcasting. Whenever oils are used, you should not touch your face or clothing with the oil on your hands. After you recite the last words of a spell, you should wash your hands thoroughly with warm water and soap. The oil is for external use only and should never be taken internally. You should not use the oil on the face or other sensitive areas. Some people experience allergic reactions to oils, so you may wish to test a small patch of skin on your arm before using the oil. If sensitivity does occur, you may anoint the plate using a cotton ball, a cotton swab, or disposable gloves.

Matches or a lighter may be used to light the candles and incense. Monitor any incense and candles until they have burned out, but you do not have to sit and watch them every minute. I do advise you should never leave a burning candle unattended, but I often do other things while my spell candles are burning. I check them frequently to avoid mishaps, but we all lead very busy lives and it is not always possible to sit for an hour or more just to watch a candle burn down.

The most frequently used candles for spellwork are as follows:

4-inch candles: will burn for approximately seventy-five to ninety minutes and are chosen because they will burn out the same evening they are lit. You may wish to burn these candles one at a time, or in a series of three, five, or seven. You can burn one candle each evening for three, five, or seven days, depending upon how much time you wish to spend on the situation.

6-inch candles: will burn for approximately four to five hours and are chosen for their longer burn time for more intense spellwork. Again, you may wish to burn these candles individually, or in a series as above.

9-inch candles: are chosen most often for use in a fourteen-day spell, burning the candle for sixty to ninety minutes each evening, and then snuffing it out. When using a candle for multiple days, one should not blow out the candle, as it is thought that the wish will blow away as well. Use a snuffer instead. On the final evening of the spell, the candle will be left to burn out on its own, within the bounds of safety.

The quartz crystal is used to absorb negative energy while performing the spell. Take the time to pick up several crystals, hold them, and see if you feel anything when you handle them. Most people instinctively know when they have chosen the right crystals for spellwork. When you find the crystal you would like to use, it is best to cleanse it prior to spellwork. The best way to do that is to soak the crystal in a salt and water mixture to cleanse it of any energy it may have absorbed from other people handling it. Another way to cleanse it is to leave it on a windowsill for up to one week in the sunlight and moonlight, preferably the week leading up to the full moon.

Any spell is more powerful when a personal item is included. To attract prosperity, the most powerful items would be coins, dollar bills, résumés for job hunting, business cards of prospective employers or customers, and related legal documents. Additionally, if you are working the spell for someone else, such as a family member or friend, you should have something of that person's to incorporate into the spell. It could be a business card, something with their signature on it, or, if you are really close, ask for some of their hair.

When using a large item, such as a résumé or legal document, it is not necessary to completely cover it with herbs, and you certainly don't want to get oil stains on it if you want to make a good impression. Place the item on the altar and sprinkle it sparingly with herbs. If you want, lightly run your fingers down the edges of the paper after you have wiped the excess oil off them with a paper towel. To prevent melted wax from ruining them, do not place the candle on top of the papers.

Additionally, a spell should be a reflection of you, so I suggest you include words of your own during any of the spell recitations. Each need is unique and only you know what it is you wish to accomplish in performing a spell. Speak directly from your heart, because there are no wrong words and there is no wrong way to perform a spell. Let your soul guide you, and know that all things are possible.

Each ingredient listed in appendix A may be used for the appropriate prosperity spells that have been noted after its name. An asterisk indicates the item is poisonous and should probably not be used except by a knowledgeable practitioner. Tobacco, which is itself poisonous and should never be ingested, may be safely substituted for any poisonous substance.

Types of Prosperity Magic Spells

The following are the most common types of spells associated with prosperity, and their uses.

Attraction: To attract money and good fortune. May also be employed when participating in games of chance, such as before buying a lottery ticket or taking a trip to the casino.

Banishing: To rid oneself of negative influences, bad habits, or offensive people. Banishing may also be employed to dispel negative feelings after a layoff or job loss of any kind.

Beginnings: Helps to get one started off on the right foot. Can be effective when dealing with a new boss, starting a new job, or starting a new business.

Blessing: To bring all the best and positive energies to all your business and work endeavors.

Communication: Helps to open up and keep lines of communication with bosses and coworkers positive and moving toward a common goal. Can also be employed when approaching a bank or investor for start-up funds.

Creativity: Aids in opening up the conscious and unconscious mind to new thoughts and ideas. Helps to get creative juices flowing.

Dispelling negativity: Helps clear away negative energy and people to keep one moving forward.

Endings: Aids in putting an end to a situation, relationship, or unhealthy work environment.

Inspiration: Brings out the best and brightest ideas in creative minds. Often used in the artistic endeavors of artists, writers, or musicians.

Job hunting: Aids in locating a job or career more to one's liking.

Legal matters: Aids one when dealing with legal matters and the court system.

Magic power: Adds more magical energy to the other items used in a spell or ritual. Like caffeine in the morning, it adds an extra kick to magic.

Overcoming obstacles: Helps one find courage to overcome obstacles or to avoid those already in place. Can aid in breaking barriers created by the individual or by others who wish to hold one back.

Peace: Can be used to bring peace to a stressful situation or to thank the gods when a situation has been resolved.

Power: Helps to put one in the driver's seat in career and business matters. Can be especially useful for small business owners and entrepreneurs just starting out.

Prosperity: Used for bringing one comfort and security in one's career. Can also be used to attract money, to get a raise, or to start a business.

Protection: Helps protect the practitioner while performing magic, as well as surrounding one with protective energy. May be useful for guarding against financial downturns and instability.

Purification: Often called cleansing, this removes unwanted and harmful energy. May be used on ritual tools, persons, or structures; it can also be helpful in clearing a road to success.

Reconciliation: Used to bring harmony to stressful situations specifically related to job hunting, career changes, or work-related disagreements.

Release: Used for those times when it is best to let go of a job, out-of-control spending habits, or negative influences and people.

Reversing: Used to send negative energy or intentions back to the sender. Can also be employed to reverse a pattern of behavior or personal financial setbacks.

Success: Aids in finding career success, launching a new business, or climbing the corporate ladder.

Sympathetic magic: The use of an item to represent an individual. It is a commonly held belief that the magic performed upon the item will affect the person or business the item represents. Including a copy of your résumé or a business card from a recruiter can boost your magic and can have a positive effect on the outcome of that next job interview. Use your imagination, because the possibilities are virtually endless.

Transitions: Helps to make changes in life easier to deal with. Can also be employed to change the dynamics of a situation from good to bad, or bad to good, depending upon the accompanying magic.

Wishes: Sometimes there's no readily available spell that covers a particular situation; in that case, a wish spell can apply to any number of situations or dreams one may have, regardless of the nature of the wish.

Oil Blending Basics

Before we start on the road to prosperity, let's get down to the basics of making magical oils. If you've glanced ahead in this book, you've probably noticed that all the spells require them. Making your own oils is usually best. In the process of blending the essential oils, herbs, and other items into the base oil, you have the opportunity to infuse the mixture with some of your energy, what you hope to accomplish, and what your needs are. This will further improve the effectiveness of your spells.

I covered much of this material in my previous book *Egyptian Revenge Spells*, but it still bears repeating. Essential oils are very potent. Some people may suffer allergic reactions to them, so always work in a well-ventilated area. The citrus oils, specifically, are photosensitive, meaning that use of them may cause skin discoloration when exposed to sunlight.

It is best to purchase true essential oils and not just fragrance oils. A true essential oil will be more costly, but a little goes a long way. Essential oils are distilled in a variety of ways from actual plant materials and carry the best fragrance, as well as the essence of the plant. I do not use essential oils like civet and musk, and substitute synthetic oil instead, so no animals will be harmed. Do your homework when purchasing oils; look for price and quantity. But remember, you don't need much; each of the recipes uses only a few drops. Essential oils do lose their potency over time; to extend shelf life, blend them with a base oil.

Base oils, also called carrier oils, are used to dilute the essential oils for ease and variety of use. An essential oil should not be used directly on the skin, but once it has been diluted properly, it may be used as a personal fragrance, a massage oil, and, as we shall be doing, for anointing candles. I have not specified a base oil for the recipes. I generally use almond, apricot, coconut, or grapeseed, as they have a light texture; these and others are listed below. You may also want to consider their price, shelf life, ease of use, and availability when making your choice.

Magical oils should always be stored in dark-colored bottles to keep them fresh; light affects the potency of all oils. It is best to keep any essential or magical oil tightly capped, in a cool, dark place, out of direct sunlight. Keep them out of the reach of children and pets, since ingestion could be fatal. Once the magical oil blend has been created, label the bottle and put the date on it. It is best to keep magical oils for up to two years and then discard.

Each recipe on the following pages is blended into one teaspoon of base oil. Take the teaspoon of base oil, pour it into a dark-colored bottle (you will probably need a small funnel), and add the essential oils of the recipe you have chosen. Tightly cap and shake well. Uncap the bottle and add herbs or any other item listed. Again, tightly cap and shake well. Finally, label it and your magical oil is ready for use.

A magical oil can be used in various creative ways, not just for anointing candles. Wear a dab when meeting a prospective employer, and use it to anoint your résumés, cover letters, and business cards. Use your imagination and have fun with the oils you create.

Common Base (Carrier) Oils

The following are the most common base oils for making magical oil blends. You can also instill a base oil with your intent. Since many of these oils are geared to prosperity, any of them would be appropriate for use.

Almond: A pale yellow oil; light textured; almost odorless.

Apricot: A darker yellow to pale orange oil; light textured.

Avocado: A pale yellow oil; a bit thicker; almost odorless.

Coconut: The oil is almost colorless and odorless; extremely light textured.

Evening primrose: A golden yellow oil; fine textured; faintly musty odor. A bit expensive and has a short shelf life.

Grapeseed: A pale green oil; no scent; light textured.

Hazelnut: An almost colorless oil; light textured, slightly greasy; nutty odor. Most often used in conjunction with another base oil.

Hemp seed: A pale yellow oil; almost odorless; light textured.

Jojoba: A golden to clear oil; odorless; light textured.

Olive: Colors range from dark green to pale golden, depending upon how refined it is; faint odor; textures range from heavy to light.

Rose hip: A pale yellow to rich orange oil; almost odorless; light textured.

Safflower: A golden yellow oil with a heavier texture; faint nutty odor.

Sesame: A clear to pale yellow oil with a heavier texture; faint bitter to nutty odor.

Sunflower: A golden yellow oil; faint sweet to nutty odor; light textured.

Wheat germ: A pale orange oil; slight earthy odor; heavier and sticky in texture. Most often used in conjunction with another base oil.

Each spell should be performed with the corresponding oil blend for the best results, but any of the following essential oils can be substituted, or can be used individually for any prosperity spells: allspice, cinnamon, five-finger grass, frankincense, lavender, myrrh, orange, patchouli, sandalwood, or vetivert. Additionally, if a need for an emergency spell arises, use of one essential oil blended with a base is perfectly acceptable. Spellwork should bring about positive results, not make the practitioner feel stressed about having the right blend.

THREE

Egyptian Deities for Spells

The Egyptian deities were different from many of the other pantheons, such as Greek and Roman, for it was believed that the gods first ruled on earth and passed along their knowledge to the people. When the gods grew old and feeble, they passed on the throne and retired to the heavens to watch over the people. Although the gods no longer ruled on earth, they were still looking on, guiding the people and providing for them.

This concept inextricably linked magic and religion in ancient Egypt, and what affected one affected all. If the Nile did not provide enough silt during the annual inundation, crop production would suffer, and all would feel the devastation. So when we look at the Egyptian deities related to prosperity, they are fertility gods, gods of the harvest or agriculture, or creation deities. The first sheaves of grain, the first bunch of grapes, the first calf slaughtered would be offered to the gods in thanks, as well as to ensure the continued beneficence of the gods.

The following deities are the most appropriate to call upon in times of financial need. They relate to creation, abundance, fertility, and harvest; also listed are deities for truth and justice. Each spell lists certain deities that may be invoked for aid. When you become adept at spellwork, you will instinctively know when to invoke a deity and which would be the best choice. I personally do not invoke deities during routine spellwork—only when the work is difficult or the need is urgent. Calling on the gods in times of financial distress may give additional emphasis to the spell, but calling on the gods each and every time you perform a spell is like crying wolf; when you really need their help, they may not be listening.

The sketches below provide a concise introduction to prosperity deities. In order to fully understand Egyptian mythology and beliefs, a great deal more study would be necessary and could realistically take months or years. I have taken the liberty of listing some related books in the bibliography, if you wish to investigate further.

Amun (Amen)

Pronunciation: Äh-mōōn (Äh-měn)

The cult of Amun, the official state deity, was perhaps the most powerful in all of Egypt. By 1160 BCE, it is estimated that one-fifth of the population, one-third of the land, and three-quarters of the wealth of Egypt belonged to the temple of Amun-Ra at Thebes. Temples were erected to his glory in all parts of Egypt. The priests of Amun held considerable political power, second only to the king, and responsibility for the smooth running of the temple complex often was passed from father to son over several generations.

Mythology: Amun, though the state deity, was also the protector of the common man, thus adding to his popularity. He was compassionate and benevolent to the poor, as well as being the protector of the king and Egypt itself. He was revered as a triad along with his wife, the goddess Mut, and their son, Khonsu. The Opet Festival celebrated the marriage of Amun and Mut. In addition to Thebes, his temple sites and cult centers

Amun

included Amada, Soleb, Abu Simbel, and Gebel Barkal. His major festival was August 18.

Correspondences: Amun was often depicted with blue flesh, alluding to his cosmic aspects. Frankincense, burned in his temples daily, was believed to be the sweat of the god. Colors appropriate for candles would be yellow, gold, orange, white, blue, green, and black.

Animals: Bull, frog, Nile goose, hawk, lion, ram, snake.

Associations: Sky god; sun god; god of wind, air, and atmosphere; creation deity; god of war; god of fertility; god of agriculture; protector of travelers.

Epithets: Lord of the Thrones of the Two Lands; Mysterious of Form; Lord of the Two Horns; the Hidden One; Fierce Red-eyed Lion; Lord of Time; One Who Made Himself into Millions.

Offerings: Gemstones such as amethyst, emerald, or sapphire; herbs such as aloe, cedarwood, cinnamon, clove, olive leaves, or saffron; resinous incenses, especially frankincense; liquids such as beer, wine, or olive oil; perfumes with musk; feathers.

Spells: Beginnings, creativity, fertility, power, protection, wishes.

Apophis

Pronunciation: Äh-pōe-fĭs

Apophis was the primeval force of darkness and chaos in ancient Egypt. Each evening, the sun god Ra sailed on his barque through the land of the dead, the Duat, to vanquish Apophis and to be reborn the following day with the rising of the sun. Apophis was associated with earthquakes and storms, and the ancients believed that, when a solar eclipse occurred, Apophis had swallowed Ra's solar barque.

Apophis

Mythology: Spitting was a reviled action, tantamount to cursing, so it is only appropriate that the most common myth surrounding this deity has him formed from the spittle of the goddess Neith. Though Ra, along with other deities, battled Apophis each night, Apophis would never be destroyed, for in so doing, the proper order of the cosmos would be destroyed as well. The birthday of Apophis is noted as February 5 and he is mentioned in regard to a festival on December 29. He does not appear to have had any cult centers of his own.

Correspondences: Colors appropriate for candles would be black, red, and white.

Animals: Crocodile, serpent, snake.

Associations: Night demon; chaos monster.

Epithets: The Evil One; Serpent of Rebirth; the Evil Lizard; the Fiend of Darkness.

Offerings: Resinous incense such as benzoin; liquids such as beer or wine.

Spells: Beginnings, breakups, cursing, dispelling negativity, endings, hexing, transitions.

Bes

Pronunciation: Bĕs (like "best" without the "t")

Bes is most often depicted as a dwarfish man, with an ugly, masklike face, tongue protruding. His statues often show him brandishing knives as a deterrent to evil spirits, making him a protective deity, and he was the protector of women in childbirth. He was sometimes depicted as a musician, playing instruments to placate the goddess Hathor, gaining him his association with music. He was a contradiction: he was jovial and belligerent, fond of dancing and fighting. However, he was a very popular deity, with his image appearing on amulets, unguent jars, headrests, mirrors, and cosmetic items, as well as temple walls, statuary, and furniture.

Mythology: His mythology is unknown, and his origins are difficult to determine; he may have been a composite of as many as ten other deities. As patron of the home, it is quite possible he was worshipped in a niche in the common Egyptian abode. Bes could be called on to ward off scorpions and snakes, and to protect against evil spirits and bad influences that could cause discord in the home. He brought good luck and prosperity to married couples. He had no official temples or cult centers.

Bes

Correspondences: Colors appropriate for candles would be black, red, white, green, and blue.

Animals: Lion.

Associations: Protector of childbirth and rebirth; god of war; patron of art and music; strangler of antelopes, bears, lions, and serpents.

Epithets: Protector of Hunters; the Warrior; Guardian of Horus; God of Dance and Music; He Who Tears out the Hearts of the Wicked.

Offerings: Black, red, or chili peppers; liquids such as beer or wine; mirrors; perfume bottles; makeup.

Spells: Attraction (love), beginnings, fertility, healing, peace, prosperity, protection, reconciliation, sex, tranquility.

Geb

Pronunciation: Gēb

Frequently mentioned in the Pyramid Texts, Geb was the personification of earth, often depicted as a reclining man lying on the ground, one knee bent, raised up on one elbow, to symbolize the hills and mountains. His

Geb

skin was green and his body was decorated with plants, showing his association with fertility. He had a darker aspect: those who did not find eternal life in the Duat were imprisoned within the earth. His laughter caused earthquakes and he could be called upon to treat headaches, scorpion stings, and snakebites.

Mythology: Geb was one of the first gods to rule Egypt, and as such the throne of Egypt was referred to as the seat of Geb. He was the son of the goddess Tefnut and the god Shu. His wife, Nut, gave birth to their children: Horus the Elder, Osiris, Set, Isis, and Nephthys. He had no major cult centers or temples. His feasts and festivals were February 15 and April 18.

Correspondences: Colors appropriate for candles would be black, blue, green, orange, white, and yellow.

Animals: Goose, hare.

Associations: God of healing; earth god; fertility god.

Epithets: Eldest of Shu; Judge in the Divine Tribunal of the Gods; Controller of the Earth Snakes; Heir of the Gods; the Great Cackler.

Offerings: Plants such as cedar, barley, or reeds; liquids such as beer or wine.

Spells: Creativity, fertility, healing, prosperity, protection.

Hapy (Hapi)
Pronunciation: Just like the word "happy"

Hapy was the personification of the annual inundation of the Nile, which started the planting season. He was closely associated with fertility, thus earning him the title Friend of Geb. The annual inundation was referred to as the arrival of Hapy. He is often depicted as a blue-skinned man with a swollen belly (abundance), pendulous breasts

Hapy

(fertility), and wearing a crown of lotus (symbol of Upper Egypt, or the south) and papyrus (symbol of Lower Egypt, or the north).

Mythology: His legends relate to the arrival of the inundation. He also had a harem of frog-headed goddesses, in keeping with his association with fertility and abundance. Hapy was the god governing the season Akhet (winter), which was the season of the inundation. He had no temples specifically dedicated to him, but he did have cult centers at Elephantine (Adu) and Gebel el-Silsila. His major festival was September 28. It is also possible he was worshipped during two other festivals: the Feast of the Nile (January 26) and the Feast of Akhet (July 25), which welcomed the rise of the Nile.

Correspondences: Colors appropriate for candles would be black, blue, green, orange, white, and yellow.

Animals: Goose.

Associations: Fertility god; creator god; god of fish and marsh birds; god of the Nile.

Epithets: Friend of Geb; Father of the Gods; Lord of Fishes and Birds of the Marsh; Master of the River

Bringing Vegetation; Lord of the Poor and Needy; Lord of the Two Lands; the One Who Greens the Two Banks; the Maker of Barley and Wheat.

Offerings: Any aquatic plants, such as papyrus and lotus, or barley and wheat; liquids such as beer, wine, or water.

Spells: Attraction (money), beginnings, creativity, fertility, prosperity, sex.

Hathor

Pronunciation: Hǎ-thôr or Hǎ-tôre

Worshipped as far back as the Old Kingdom, Hathor was celebrated as the mother of the king. The feast of Hathor was exceedingly popular, with its alcohol and merriment (a drunken orgy in actuality); her temple at Dendera was known as the house of intoxication. Hathor could also be identified as seven cows, called the Seven Hathors (Goddesses of Fate), which determined the destiny of a child at birth. In addition, it was Hathor who provided celestial food to the deceased and kept watch over the Theban necropolis.

Hathor

She cared for the dead and presided over both heaven and the underworld.

Mythology: Hathor was the wife of Horus the Elder, and as such, both were worshipped along with their son Ihy, the sistrum player, at Edfu and Dendera. The annual festival in honor of their marriage lasted fourteen days. The sistrum, a kind of rattle, was associated with Hathor and was used extensively in her festivals. Many sistra have been unearthed that were carved in her likeness. As the daughter of Ra, she was sometimes equated with Sekhmet in the destruction of mankind when they disrespected Ra. Her terror upon the earth was only satiated when fields were flooded with beer tinted red like blood, which she drank until unable to carry out further slaughter. Hathor has also been identified as the mother of Horus the Younger, though that role is most often associated with Isis. Hathor governed the month of Hethara, the third month in the winter season of Akhet (Inundation). The festival of Hathor was approximately November 27. Her temples and cult centers included Dendera (Yunet), Edfu, Thebes, and Memphis. Locations outside of Egypt were a testament to her popularity, including sites in Byblos, Nubia, and the Sinai Peninsula. The birthday of Hathor is noted as August 29. Feasts and festivals to her were January 4 and 23, April

1, May 15 and 19, June 16, July 22 and 23, August 7, September 17 and 21, October 4, 21, and 29, November 2 and 28, and December 23.

Correspondences: Colors appropriate for candles would be red, gold, yellow, white, silver, turquoise, black, and blue.

Animals: Cat, cobra, cow, falcon, hawk, lioness, snake.

Associations: Creation deity; patroness of lovers; goddess of sexual love; goddess of foreign lands; sun goddess; moon goddess; sky goddess; goddess of the afterlife; funerary goddess; goddess of women and family; mother goddess; goddess of moisture and vegetation; goddess of makeup; goddess of joy, music, happiness, dance, drunkenness, and song; goddess of myrrh.

Epithets: House of Horus; Mistress of the Red Cloth; Lady of the Necropolis; Mistress of Turquoise; the Golden One; the Beautiful One; Lady of the Southern Sycamore; Eye of Ra; Queen of the West; Lady of Fragrance; Lady of the Stars.

Offerings: Gemstones such as turquoise or emerald; herbs such as papyrus, sycamore, mandrake, rose, myrtle, clover, or patchouli; resinous incenses such as benzoin, myrrh, or sandalwood; liquids such as beer, wine, milk, or water; heavily fragranced perfumes; makeup; feathers.

Spells: Attraction (love), beginnings, bewitching, creativity, cursing, dispelling negativity, healing, love, lust, passion, power, protection, purification, sex, transitions.

Heqet

Pronunciation: Hĕck-ĕt

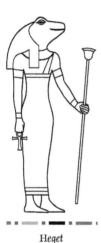

Heqet

First mentioned in the Pyramid Texts, Heqet presided as midwife over the conception and birth of children in ancient Egypt. She is most often depicted as a frog-headed woman, as the frog was a symbol of new life and fecundity. Many women wore or carried a frog amulet to guarantee fertility, and magical ivory knives, another symbol of the goddess, would be kept in the birthing room. It is quite possible that "the servants of Heqet" was a term used for the midwives who assisted in childbirth.

Mythology: Heqet gained more of a connection to childbirth in the Middle Kingdom, and it is said she assisted Isis in bringing Osiris back to life in order to conceive the god Horus. She is often identified as the consort of the god Khnum. Her temples were at Qus and Her-wer.

Correspondences: Colors appropriate for candles would be black, blue, green, orange, white, and yellow.

Animals: Frog.

Associations: Patron goddess of childbirth.

Epithets: Mistress of Joy; Lady of Her-wer; Mistress of the Two Lands; Defender of the Home; She Who Fills the Ka with the Breath of Life.

Offerings: Any aquatic plants, such as lotus, reeds, or papyrus; liquids such as beer, wine, milk, or water; any frog statue.

Spells: Beginnings, creativity, protection, transitions.

Horus
Pronunciation: Hôar-ŭs

As the ultimate symbol of divine kingship, Horus was already established in pre-dynastic Egypt. All rulers were perceived as the "living Horus" on the throne by the unification of Upper and Lower Egypt (c. 3000 BCE). In the Pyramid Texts, Horus is the god who is called upon to perform the Opening of the Mouth ceremony on the dead king, assuring the ascension to the throne of

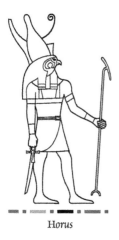
Horus

the next "living Horus." If a king died without heirs, the male who presided over the Opening of the Mouth ceremony at the burial was generally assured the throne and became Horus on earth.

Mythology: Horus is most commonly identified as the son of Isis and the dead Osiris, but he has various forms and related mythologies. As Horus the Elder, he is the son of Geb and Nut, brother of Isis, Osiris, Nephthys, and Set. As Horus of Edfu, he is the son of Ra, husband of Hathor and father of Ihy. He was protector of the king, a symbol of resurrection, and the representation of light, while Set was the representation of dark. In later texts, these attributes are ascribed to Horus, son of Isis (also Horus the Younger). As Horus the Younger, he is the son of Hathor and Horus of Edfu, uniter of the Two Lands. Horus is further identified as the father of four sons, guardians of the internal organs of the mummy, who are named Duamutef, Hapi, Imsety, and Qebhsennuf. Horus is the guardian of the second month, Payni, of the summer (harvest) season, Shemu. His temples and cult centers included Buto, Edfu, Abydos, Letopolis, Heliopolis, Nekhen, Khem, Kom Ombo, and Pharbocthos, as well as the Nubian towns of Baki, Buhen, and Miam. The birthday of Horus the Elder is noted as July 15, while the birthday of Horus, son of Isis, is noted as December 25. Feasts and festivals to this god in his various forms were January 6 and 15, February 6, 18, and 21, March 15 and 16, April 14, 15, and 20, May 29, June 13 and 26, July 23, August 17, 19, 24, and 31, September 6, 16, 24 and 26, October 13 and 14, and November 2, 15, 16, and 25.

Correspondences: Colors appropriate for candles would be orange, yellow, gold, blue, white, black, green, and red.

Animals: Crocodile, falcon, hawk, Egyptian mongoose, lion, serpent, shrew-mouse.

Associations: Sky god; sun god; creation deity; patron deity of Lower Egypt.

Epithets: Lord of the Sky; the Distant One; the Pillar of his Mother; Lord of the Two Lands; the Lancer; God of the East.

Offerings: Gemstones such as ruby or any red stones; herbs such as black pepper, oak, nettle, rue, wormwood, or tobacco; resinous incenses such as dragon's blood or myrrh; liquids such as beer or wine; sulfur; feathers.

Spells: Beginnings, creativity, cursing, dispelling negativity, overcoming obstacles, power, prosperity, protection, reconciliation, revenge, transitions.

Imhotep

Pronunciation: Ĭm-hōe-tĕp

Most often depicted as a seated scribe with the shaved head of a priest and a scroll of papyrus on his lap, Imhotep was one of the few humans (mortals) so revered by the people that he was deified about two thousand years after his death. He was an architect, master sculptor, priest, scribe, sage, physician, chief vizier, and author of a book of instruction under the Third Dynasty King Djoser. He has been credited with the invention of architecture in stone, and in c. 2670 BCE built the first pyramid in history, the Step Pyramid at Saqqara.

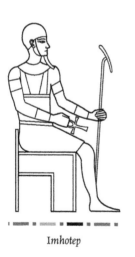

Imhotep

Mythology: Imhotep, as son of Ptah, was worshipped as a god of healing and architecture. In some myths he has replaced the god Nefertem as the son of

Ptah and Sekhmet. His temples and cult centers included Saqqara, Thebes, and Philae.

Correspondences: Colors appropriate for candles would be green, blue, white, red, and black.

Animals: Although Imhotep was never depicted in animal form, mummified ibises were offered to him at his temple at Saqqara.

Associations: God of healing, medicine, wisdom, and learning; patron of writing; role model for scribes; protector of those occupied with sciences and occult arts; patron of doctors.

Epithets: The Great Physician; He Who Comes in Peace; Scribe of the Gods; Overseer of Works; the Skillful Fingered One; He Who Brought Healing to Mankind; He Who Gives Life to All Men.

Offerings: Herbs such lavender; any resinous incense; liquids such as beer or wine; almonds; any writing instrument.

Spells: Creativity, healing, inspiration, magic, power, spirituality.

Isis
Pronunciation: Ī-sĭs

Isis was the symbolic mother of the king, making her the most revered goddess in ancient Egypt. With her husband

Osiris, she taught the people to grind corn, spin flax, and weave cloth, and passed on her knowledge of healing.

Isis

She was the ideal of fidelity and, during her rule with her husband, brought prosperity, fertility, and peace to Egypt. When Osiris left Egypt to bring civilization to the world, she ruled as a beneficent queen and taught the people all they would need to domesticate animals, raise crops, and provide for themselves. Her veneration extended far beyond her own country, as she was assimilated into Greek and Roman mythology as well. Her worship survived even beyond the Egyptian empire, only ending when the Roman emperor Justinian in 551 CE closed her temple at Philae, the seat of the last of the Egyptian pagan cults.

Mythology: Isis was the daughter of Geb and Nut, sister of Nephthys, Set, and Horus the Elder, and sister-wife of Osiris. As a selfless act, she raised Anubis, the son of Nephthys and Osiris; Nephthys had bewitched Osiris by appearing to him in the guise of Isis in order to conceive a child. It is interesting to note that while Isis was a popular goddess with the people, she had no temples dedicated to her alone until late in Egyptian history, though each temple constructed had a section of it set aside for her worship. Her temples and cult centers included Giza, Behbeit el-Hagar, Dier el-Shelwit (Thebes), Abydos, Dendera, Perehbet, and Philae, as well as sites outside Egypt at Byblos, Acropolis (Athens), Delos, and Pompeii. The festival celebrating the marriage of Isis and Osiris was noted as July 19. The birthday of Isis was celebrated July 17; her feasts and festivals were January 7 and 8, March 23, August 12 and 18, September 1 and 24, October 3 and 10, November 24, 25, and 29, and December 21 and 31.

Correspondences: Colors appropriate for candles would be silver, white, black, green, blue, yellow, orange, gold, and red.

Animals: Cat, cow, hawk, kite, scorpion, snake, sow, swallow, vulture.

Associations: Moon goddess; earth goddess; goddess of cultivated lands and fields; goddess of magical power; patron of women and marriage; giver of life.

Epithets: Great of Magic; the Mighty One; Goddess of the Sea; Mistress of the World in the Beginning; Foremost of the Goddesses; the Throne Goddess; Mistress of the Pyramid; Lady of Heaven, Earth, and the Netherworld; Eye of Ra; Clever of Tongue; the Great Enchantress.

Offerings: Gemstones such as ruby, turquoise, sapphire, star sapphire, pearls, amethyst, peridot, aquamarine, or crystal; herbs such as narcissus, lavender, rose geranium, vervain, lotus, lily of the valley, cedarwood, olive leaves, orris, poppy, rose, sycamore, wormwood, or cypress; resinous incenses such as myrrh or dragon's blood; liquids such as olive oil, beer, wine, or milk; perfumes with civet or musk; feathers.

Spells: Beginnings, bewitching, breakups, creativity, grief, healing, hexing, jealousy, love, magic, power, prosperity, protection, revenge, reversing.

Khepri
Pronunciation: Kĕp-rē

The god Khepri was the sun at dawn, pushing the sun disk across the sky, thus equated with the scarab beetle, pushing its ball of dung from the silt of the Nile. Scarab amulets were worn to obtain the power of the god, and were buried with the dead in the mummy wrappings to assure the dead of resurrection in the Underworld. These scarab amulets were most often colored blue (lapis lazuli), associating Khepri with the heavens, or black, associating him with fertility and the earth.

Mythology: Khepri is most commonly portrayed as the creator of Shu, god of air, and his twin sister Tefnut, goddess of moisture. These two deities personified the first concepts to emerge from the chaos to create all the other gods. Khepri was the guardian of the spring season (Peret), which was the sowing season. His main temple and cult center was in Heliopolis. The major festival to Khepri was March 1.

Khepri

Correspondences: Colors appropriate for candles would be orange, yellow, gold, black, blue, green, and white.

Animals: Scarab beetle.

Associations: Sun god; god of resurrection and fertility; creation deity.

Epithets: Beetle God of Dawn; Controller of Celestial Motion; the One Who is in the Primeval Waters; the Shining One; He Who Emerges from the Earth; the One Who Created Himself.

Offerings: Herbs such as lotus or poppy; resinous incense such as benzoin; liquids such as beer, wine, or water; scarab beetle amulets.

Spells: Beginnings, creativity, endings, fertility, grief, protection, transitions, wishes.

Khnum

Pronunciation: Cŏ-nōōm

Worshipped in the early dynastic period, Khnum is credited with fashioning both gods and men on his potter's wheel. He presides over the creation of children in the womb and infuses them with health. As guardian of the Nile, Khnum brings forth the annual inundation. He is most often depicted as a ram-headed man, working at his potter's wheel.

Mythology: As with many deities in Egypt, Khnum's mythology is confusing. He is sometimes the husband of the goddess Neith; however, his most enduring connection is with the goddess Heqet, for it is Khnum who assists her at the birth of all children. He appears to have had three wives: Heqet, Anukis (possibly a Sudanese goddess), and Satis, his daughter by Anukis. Khnum had cult centers at Elephantine (Adu), Esna, Her-wer, and Shashotep. His feasts and festivals were January 22, July 27, and August 16 and 26.

Khnum

Correspondences: Colors appropriate for candles would be black, blue, green, orange, white, and yellow.

Animals: Ram.

Associations: Creator god; god of water; sun god; god of fertility.

Epithets: Lord of the Crocodiles; High of Plumes, Sharp of Horns; Lord of the Cataract; the Potter God; the Divine Craftsman; Lord of the Wheel; the One Who Fashions Gods and Men; Potter of Mankind; Nile God of All Egypt; Lord of the Land of Life.

Offerings: Liquids such as beer, wine, or water; clay.

Spells: Beginnings, creativity, fertility, healing, power, prosperity, spirituality.

Ma'at
Pronunciation: Mäy-äht or Mä-äht

Ma'at is the personification of stability and balance in Egyptian cosmology, as well as the physical and moral law of the universe. She is the ultimate judge in the Underworld; all dead have their hearts weighed against the feather of Ma'at. If one has lived a just and upright life, his heart will be lighter than her feather and he may enjoy eternal life. Judges were referred to as "priests of Ma'at." She is most often depicted as a kneeling woman wearing an ostrich feather on her head.

Ma'at

Mythology: As the daughter of Ra, Ma'at regulates the path of the sun and assists Ra each day as he travels the sky. In order to keep cosmic order, a figurine of Ma'at was presented to the local or state god in each temple in Egypt. Her main cult center and temple was at Thebes. Her feasts and festivals were April 3 and 4, May 30, June 1 and 15, October 7 and 8, and November 28.

Correspondences: Colors appropriate for candles would be black, blue, green, orange, white, and yellow.

Animals: None.

Associations: Goddess of justice; goddess of law; goddess of truth; goddess of cosmic harmony and moral integrity.

Epithets: Beloved Daughter of Ra; She of the Beautiful Face; Controller of the Seasons; Food of the Gods; Lady of Heaven; Queen of the Earth; Mistress of the Underworld; Eye of Ra.

Offerings: Gemstones such as emerald; herbs such as aloe; liquids such as galbanum oil, beer, or wine; feathers (especially ostrich).

Spells: Beginnings, endings, legal matters, power, protection, purification, transitions.

Min

Pronunciation: Mĭn (like "in")

Reference to Min can be found as far back as c. 3000 BCE. Although little is known of his origins, his cult was one of the oldest and most widespread. He could quite possibly be a foreign god who was adopted by the Egyptians. He is the supreme symbol of sexual procreativity, and is always depicted as a standing man, phallus erect, wearing a double plumed headdress. He holds the royal flagellum (whip), and his right arm is raised to strike down his enemies. As protector of travelers and roads, he was often invoked by caravan leaders before setting out across the desert.

Min

Mythology: New Kingdom festivals to Min were times for celebration, emphasizing fertility and regeneration. Min would be honored at these festivals with the first sheaf of crops as an offering for his bounty, and sistra would be rattled to frighten away demons. He was the guardian of the first month (Tybi) in the spring season (Peret), which was the season for sowing. He also may have been worshipped during the Harvest Festival on March 21. His temples and cult centers included Koptos (Gebtu), Akhmim (Ipu), Edfu, Panopolis, Kmentmin, and Qift. Feasts and festivals to Min were January 10, February 20, June 18, July 11, and October 1.

Correspondences: Some of the statues of Min are colored black, indicative of his fertile nature. He was also the master of lapis lazuli and malachite. Colors appropriate for candles would be black, green, blue, white, and red.

Animals: Falcon, lion, white bull.

Associations: God of fertility; god of vegetation (crops); god of roads and travelers; bringer of rain.

Epithets: Lord of Awe; Lord of the Eastern Desert; Ruler of the Nubian Bowmen; High of Plumes; Rich with Perfume; Great of Love; Protector of Travelers and Crops.

Offerings: Plants such as corn, flowers, lettuce, wheat, or palm; liquids such as beer or wine; heavily fragranced perfumes; feathers.

Spells: Blessings, creativity, fertility, prosperity, protection, reversing, sex.

Montu

Pronunciation: Mŏn-twō

Montu was the personification of the destructive heat of the sun. As god of war, he was protector of the king in battle. He not only assisted the living king, but also fought against the enemies of the gods.

Mythology: The Buchis bull was the living image of the god Montu. His temples and cult centers included three locations at Thebes, namely Tod, Armant, and Medamud, as well as Iuny and Hermonthis. The major festivals to Montu were February 25 and August 22.

Correspondences: Colors appropriate for candles would be orange, yellow, gold, white, red, and black.

Animals: Buchis bull, falcon, griffin, hawk.

Associations: Sun god; god of war.

Epithets: War God of Thebes; He of the Strong Arm; Eager Bull; He Who Kills the Enemies of Ra; Swooping Falcon; Lord of Djerit.

Montu

Offerings: Gemstones such as ruby or any red stones; herbs such as geranium, rue, black pepper, or wormwood;

resinous incense such as dragon's blood; liquids such as beer or wine; feathers.

Spells: Inspiration, overcoming obstacles, power, protection.

Mut

Pronunciation: Mōōt

Mut's name in Egyptian means "mother" and therefore "mother of the king." She is depicted as a woman wearing the vulture headdress of protection, often surmounted by the double crown of unified Egypt; her dress is either blue or red, in a feather pattern. She is

frequently identified with Egyptian queens and many of the New Kingdom queens adopted the vulture headdress as their own. Her earliest representation appears around 1700 BCE.

Mythology: Mut is the wife of Amun and the adoptive mother of Montu. In later myths, the adopted son is Khonsu. She is sometimes associated with Bast and offerings of cat statues have been found in excavations. Mut appears at all major temples of Amun, had sanctuaries at Heliopolis, Giza,

Mut

Tanis, and Thebes, and was unique in that she had a temple oracle. Her sanctuary at Thebes was in continual use for two thousand years. Her feasts and festivals were June 12 and August 18.

Correspondences: Colors appropriate for candles would be black, blue, green, orange, white, and yellow.

Animals: Cat, eagle, lioness, vulture.

Associations: Sky goddess; mother goddess; goddess of healing.

Epithets: Queen of the Gods; Great Mother; Mistress of Megeb; Mistress of the Nine Bows; Eye of Ra; Far Wandering Goddess; Lady of Isheru.

Offerings: Gemstones such as agate, opal, pearl, or star sapphire; herbs such as aspen, cypress, sycamore, or poppy; resinous incense such as myrrh; liquids such as beer, wine, or milk; perfumes such as civet or galbanum.

Spells: Creativity, power, prosperity, protection.

Nephthys
Pronunciation: Něf-thĭs (like "thistle")

The goddess Nephthys is an enigma. She had no cult centers, no formal worship, and no real mythology. She is most often associated with dark magic and death, and the magical use of illusion. She is protector of the king in conjunction with her sister, Isis. She symbolizes life after death and it is her hair that becomes the mummy wrappings. Nephthys seems to represent the dark aspects of

Nephthys

life, whereas her sister Isis personifies light and the living. She is most often depicted as a woman wearing a rectangular headdress surmounted by her emblem, a wicker basket. She is one of the goddesses who guard the canopic jars and sarcophagi, along with Isis, Neith, and Serqet.

Mythology: Little of her own mythology exists and Nephthys is most often relegated to a lesser role in the Osirian myth, that of assisting Isis in mourning and the burial of the dead god-king Osiris. She is the daughter of Geb and Nut, sister-wife of Set, and sister to Isis, Osiris, and Horus the Elder. She had no formal cult centers and was worshipped in conjunction with Isis or other deities. The birthday of Nephthys is noted as July 18 and her feasts coincide with those of other deities on October 3 and 10 and November 29.

Correspondences: Colors appropriate for candles would be white, silver, black, green, blue, and red.

Animals: Hawk, kite, snake, vulture.

Associations: Goddess of darkness, decay, and death; protector goddess; healing deity; funerary goddess; goddess of weaving.

Epithets: She of the Bed of Life; Lady of the House; She Who is Skilled in Magic and Words of Power; Mistress of the Gods; Lady of Life; Lady of Heaven; She of the East Wind; Mistress of the Two Lands; She of the Linen Wrappings; Protectress of the Dead.

Offerings: Gemstones such as star sapphire, ruby, crystal, or pearls; herbs such as tobacco, cypress, poppy, oak, or nettle; resinous incense such as myrrh; liquids such as beer, wine, or milk; perfumes with civet; silver; sulfur; feathers.

Spells: Bewitching, cursing, dark magic, grief, protection.

Osiris

Pronunciation: Ōh-sīgh-rĭs (like "risk")

When Osiris became king on earth, Egypt was primarily a disorganized collection of nomadic hunting tribes always at war with each other. With his wife Isis by his side, he showed the Egyptians how to survive as a civilized nation. He founded temples, provided laws, constructed towns for the people to live in, and formulated rituals for worship. Osiris taught agriculture and construction of agricultural tools and implements, how to grind wheat to make bread, how to grow grapes to make wine, and how to brew beer from barley. When he was satisfied with his work, he put Isis on the throne of Egypt to rule in his absence and traveled with the gods Anubis, Thoth, and Wepwawet to bring civilization to the world. He is most

often depicted as a mummified man with green skin, thus associating him with fertility, vegetation, and resurrection.

Mythology: Though originally a local earth and vegetation deity, Osiris evolved into one of the most beloved of all the gods. He was the son of Geb and Nut, brother of Set, Nephthys, and Horus the Elder, and husband-brother of Isis. His associations

Osiris

with death and resurrection were played out in the mummification rituals. When the reigning king died, he was said to become Osiris and join the dead god, passing his throne on to his son, the incarnation of Horus on earth. His temples and cult centers included Busiris, Abydos, Biga, Thebes, and Philae. The birthday of Osiris was noted as July 14. His feasts and festivals are numerous: January 1, 3, 20, and 25, February 10, 11, 13, and 26, March, 14, 15, and 25, April 14, May 2, June 14 and 15, August 1, 2, 5, 8, 11, 12, 17, 18, and 22, September 2, 5, 16, 28, and 29, October 3, 10, and 27, November 6, 15, and 24, and December 21.

Correspondences: Colors appropriate for candles would be orange, yellow, gold, black, green, silver, white, and red.

Animals: Apis bull, benu bird, hawk, ram.

Associations: Earth god; sun god; moon god; god of the dead; god of death and resurrection; funerary god; god of vegetation; god of fertility; lord of wine.

Epithets: The Mighty One; Possessor of Ma'at; One True of Voice; Foremost of the Westerners; Judge of the Dead; the One Whose Body Did Not Decay; Lord of the Universe; the Black One; the Perfect One.

Offerings: Gemstones such as topaz or crystal; herbs such as willow, acacia, orris, lily, ivy, lily of the valley, or tamarisk; resinous incense such as myrrh or storax; liquids such as beer or wine; feathers.

Spells: Beginnings, creativity, endings, fertility, grief, legal matters, prosperity, sex, transitions.

Ptah

Pronunciation: P-täw (soft "p" as in "paw")

Though he had very little role in the funerary cults or in the Underworld, it was Ptah who performed the Opening of the Mouth ceremony upon the gods when he created them. He was always represented as a mummified man, standing erect, holding a scepter, head covered with a skull-cap, sometimes colored blue, and his flesh was gold. The Apis bull was the physical manifestation of the god on earth, and his importance in the Egyptian pantheon was only surpassed by Amun, Ra, and Osiris. Ptah was a friend of the common man, listening to petitions, and it was he who determined individual destiny.

Mythology: Ptah was worshipped with his consort Sekhmet and her son Nefertem. After his deification, Imhotep became the son of Ptah and was worshipped alongside him in his temple. Ptah brings all things into existence by speaking, for all is created by him from his heart and tongue. Ptah was the guardian of the second month (Paopi) in the winter season (Akhet), which was the season of the inundation. His priests were

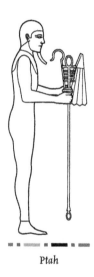

Ptah

called "master builders." His temples and cult centers included Memphis, Thebes, and Abu Simbel. Feasts and festivals to Ptah were January 6, March 15, July 12 and 13, September 5, October 15, November 16, and December 16.

Correspondences: Ptah is associated with the moringa tree. Colors appropriate for candles would be gold, blue, black, green, and white.

Animals: Apis bull.

Associations: Earth god; god of craftsmanship; creation deity; god of truth; god of artists and artisans; god of masons and blacksmiths; inventor of the arts.

Epithets: Sculptor of the Earth; the Ancient One; Lord of Ankh-Tawy; He of the Hearing Ear; Lord of Truth; He Who is Beautiful of Face; He Who Smelted the Two Lands; Hearer of Prayers.

Offerings: Gemstones such as diamonds; liquids such as beer or wine; almonds.

Spells: Beginnings, creativity, legal matters, power, spirituality, transitions, wishes.

Renenutet

Pronunciation: Wrĕn-ĕn-ōō-tĕt

Renenutet was so important at harvest time that shrines were erected in the fields during the harvesting, as well as when pressing grapes. She was guardian of the king and her gaze could vanquish enemies, yet she had a protective, nurturing nature, with her greatest concern being the nourishment of children. Renenutet kept watch over the Theban necropolis, furnished mummy

Renenutet

wrappings and, in later texts, controlled human destiny. She is sometimes depicted as a snake with a solar disk on her head.

Mythology: Renenutet had a son, Nepri, a corn deity. She may have been identified with Ma'at in the Valley of the Kings, earning her the title of Lady of Justification. Renenutet was the guardian of the fourth month (Parmuti) in the spring season (Peret), which was the sowing season. Her feasts and festivals occurred in the last month of Peret and the first month of Shemu (the spring-summer season). Her temples and cult centers were at Faiyum, Dja, Kom Abu Billo, and Terenuthis; she was also worshipped in Edfu, Dendera, Giza, Abydos, and Thebes.

Correspondences: Colors appropriate for candles would be black, blue, green, orange, white, and yellow.

Animals: Cobra, snake.

Associations: Mother goddess; goddess of harvests and childbirth; fertility goddess.

Epithets: Lady of the Fertile Land; Divine Nurse; Mistress of the Threshing Floor; Lady of Justification; Mistress of the Robes; Lady of the Granaries; Mistress of Provisions; the Snake Who Nourishes.

Offerings: Any grains; grapes; liquids such as beer, wine, or milk.

Spells: Fertility, healing, luck, power, prosperity, protection.

Sekhmet
Pronunciation: Sĕc-mĕt (like "second")

Most of the attributes of Sekhmet deal with conquest and destruction. She was the great and terrible lioness who belched fire; she could be punitive, but most often dealt death to her enemies. Her weapons were arrows, her hot breath the desert winds, and a fiery glow emanated from her body. She represented the destructive power of the sun, but her knowledge of sorcery was so great it also made her a healing goddess. Sekhmet is most often depicted as a woman with the head of a lioness.

Mythology: Sekhmet was the consort of Ptah and the mother of the god Nefertem. She is often associated with the goddesses Bast and Hathor, and shares some of their attributes. As daughter of Ra, Sekhmet almost destroyed mankind when they turned their backs on Ra. She was tricked into stopping her slaughter when the people flooded a field with beer, stained red like blood; when she drank it, she fell into a drunken stupor. To keep her fury in check, she was placated with offerings during the five Epagomenal Days, known as the birthdays of Osiris, Isis, Set, Nephthys, and Horus. Sekhmet was the guardian of the fourth month (Koiak) in the winter season (Akhet), the season of the inundation, as well as being the guardian of the east. The festival of Sekhmet was celebrated on approximately January 7. Her temples and cult centers included Heliopolis and Memphis. Her feasts and festivals were March 12, July 21, August 12, October 17 and 31, November 1, 16, 20, 24, and 28, and December 14, 28, and 31.

Correspondences: Colors appropriate for candles would be red, orange, yellow, gold, green, white, and black.

Animals: Cat, lioness.

Associations: Sun goddess; goddess of war, plagues, and pestilence; healing goddess; protectress of physicians and veterinarians.

Epithets: Lady of the Mountains of the Setting Sun; the Powerful One; Smiter of the Nubians; the Dangerous Goddess; Mistress of Life; Mistress of the Bright Red Linen; She Who Dances on Blood; Great of Magic; Lady of the Acacia; Eye of Ra; the One Who Wields the Knife.

Offerings: Herbs such as acacia or pomegranate; resinous incense such as sandalwood; liquids such as beer or wine.

Spells: Dispelling negativity, endings, healing, hexing, magic, overcoming obstacles, power, protection, revenge, transitions.

Sekhmet

Seshat
Pronunciation: Sĕy-shät (like "sat")

From the Second Dynasty onward, Seshat was called on to set the temple boundaries, known as "stretching the cord." Her role was to document the royal jubilees, to calculate the number of years a king would reign and record them on the leaves of the persea tree, and to draw up building plans as chief archivist. Seshat was also entrusted with recording the spoils of war. She is most often depicted as a woman wearing a seven-pointed star upon her head.

Mythology: Most often portrayed as the wife of Thoth, Seshat is his female counterpart in books, libraries, and writing, for it is she who records the deeds of the king. She did not have any cult centers or temples dedicated to her worship.

Correspondences: Seshat is associated with the persea tree. Colors appropriate for candles would be white, silver, blue, black, and red.

Animals: None.

Associations: Moon goddess; star goddess; goddess of writing; goddess of the library; goddess of literature;

goddess of science and mathematics; trustee of architectural drawings; patroness of architecture and astronomy; protectress of scribes and schoolchildren.

Epithets: Foremost in the Library; the Female Scribe; Lady of the Builders; the Seven-Pointed One; Keeper of the Royal Annals; Mistress of the Books; She Who Measured Time; Recorder of Deeds; Lady of the House of Books.

Seshat

Offerings: Liquids such as beer or wine; any writing or architectural instruments.

Spells: Creativity, inspiration, legal matters.

Set (Seth)
Pronunciation: Sĕt (Sĕth)

Set (along with Apophis) was the most reviled of the gods. However, many of the Nineteenth Dynasty rulers took the name of Seti, honoring his warrior nature. Set had his own creature, called the Set animal, which resembled an ass (a despised creature) with long ears and the snout of a jackal. Set's flesh was deathly white and his hair was flaming red, the color associated with the desert and evil. The ancient Egyptians felt red-haired people were distrustful and any red-coated animals were servants of Set. His allies were other despised creatures, such as the hippopotamus, crocodile, and serpent. Somewhat incongruously, Set was also a god of wine, which seems at odds with his other aspects.

Mythology: Set was worshipped in Egypt since predynastic times and was one of the oldest deities. Since he was associated with foreigners, it is quite possible he was originally a foreign god the Egyptians adopted as their own. Though the enemy of all the gods, Set was the protective patron of Upper Egypt, where he was considered a beneficent friend of the dead. In his more horrific aspects, he is the personification of drought, darkness, perversity, strife, evil, and all that is unclean. His cult centers and temples were at Memphis, Nebet, and Ombos-Naqada. The birthday of Set is noted as July 16 and his feasts and festivals were January 3, 17, and 18, March 2, August 12, 13, and 14, September 6 and 26, October 9, 12, and 13, and December 18 and 29.

Correspondences: Colors appropriate for candles would be red, black, purple, white, silver, and gold.

Animals: Antelope, ass, boar, bull, crocodile, donkey, fish, goat, hippopotamus, leopard, oryx, panther, pig, Set animal.

Set

Associations: God of thunder; god of chaos; god of violence and confusion; god of wine; god of the desert and foreign lands; god of evil and darkness; god of the unclean; protective patron god of Upper Egypt.

Epithets: The Red One; He of the Gold Town; Lord of Metals; Enemy of All the Gods; He Who Causes Storms and Clouds; the Usurper; the Disturber; Great of

Strength in the Boat of Millions; He Who Rules the Red Land of the Deserts.

Offerings: Gemstones such as black diamonds; herbs such as hemp, orris, or thistle; liquids such as beer or wine; any metals; perfumes with civet or musk.

Spells: Banishing, bewitching, binding, breakups, hexing, lust, overcoming obstacles, power, protection, revenge, sex.

Sobek
Pronunciation: Sō-bĕk (like "peck")

The Nile issued from the sweat of Sobek, in his aspect as god of water. As a creation deity, he acquired solar attributes in the form of Sobek-Ra. He is most often depicted as a crocodile, which was the personification of the powers of evil and death to the ancient Egyptians.

Mythology: Sobek is most often identified as the son of Neith, and is sometimes identified as the husband of Hathor and father of Khonsu. The birthday of Sobek is noted as December 26. His temples and cult centers included Faiyum, Crocodilopolis, Shedet, and Kom Ombo. His feasts and festivals were March 29, July 25 and 29, August 4, and October 20.

Correspondences: Colors appropriate for candles would be orange, yellow, gold, blue, red, green, black, and white.

Animals: Crocodile.

Associations: Creation deity; god of water; sun god; guardian of marshes, lakes, and rivers.

Epithets: The Raging One; the Rebel; Lord of the Floating Islands; Green of Plume; Lord of the Nile; One Who Greens the Two Banks; Lord of the Marsh; the One with the Beautiful Face; One Who Rose out of the Primeval Waters.

Sobek

Offerings: Gemstones such as carnelian; herbs such as marjoram; any aquatic plants; liquids such as beer, wine, or water.

Spells: Creativity, cursing, dispelling negativity, fertility, overcoming obstacles, power, protection, reconciliation.

Sokar

Pronunciation: Sō-cär

Sokar mixed the sacred oils and resins required in rituals and ceremonies of the gods. As a craftsman, he fashioned the grave goods for the deceased. He was also the guardian of the door to the Underworld. As god of fertility and vegetation, Sokar cuts the first clod of Nile silt to begin the planting season. His association with the Memphis necropolis dates back to pre-dynastic times, making him one of the older deities.

Mythology: The festival of Sokar, celebrated on the eve of the winter sowing, would see his image drawn through the fields on a sledge to ensure fertile land, a bountiful harvest, and prosperity for all. He was the patron god of the Memphis necropolis, where he was worshipped, but he also had a temple at Thebes. His feasts and festivals were January 11, March 15, July 12, October 20, and November 16.

Sokar

Correspondences: Colors appropriate for candles would be white, silver, black, and green.

Animals: Falcon, hawk.

Associations: God of death and the dead; funerary god; craftsman god; patron of goldsmiths; earth god; fertility god; god of vegetation.

Epithets: Lord of the Mysterious Region; Guardian of the Tombs; the Cutter; the Creator of Royal Bones; Lord of the Netherworld; Great God with his Two Wings Open.

Offerings: Liquids such as beer or wine; silver or metals; feathers.

Spells: Beginnings, creativity, endings, fertility, power, transitions.

Thoth

Pronunciation: Thôth (like "sloth")

Thoth is an important deity said to have invented the arts and sciences, music and magic, astronomy, medicine, surgery, divination, and hieroglyphs, which were thought to be the words of the gods. He devised the lunar calendar to fix the dates of the temple festivals. As one of the divine judges in the afterlife, one of his duties in the Underworld was to grant eternal life to the deceased, if they were found worthy. Thoth took part in the creation of the world and helped to turn the thoughts of Ra into material objects. He is most often depicted as an ibis-headed man, standing, with a scribe's reed and palette in hand. Scribes, by virtue of their profession, were called "the followers of Thoth" and were considered a privileged class.

Thoth

Mythology: Identified as the son of Ra, Thoth is most often paired with the goddess Seshat, who assists him in the library. He was the guardian of the first month (Thuthi) in the winter season (Akhet), which was the season of the inundation. His temples and cult centers included Esna, Saqqara (Khemnu), Nubia, the Dakhleh oasis, and the Sinai, thus his followers controlled the turquoise mines of the region. His feasts and festivals were January 24, 26, and 27, April 3, May 14, July 19, August 6, 19, and 20, October 12, 23, and 25, November 12, and December 13 and 14.

Correspondences: Red and black ink were the palette colors used by scribes. Colors appropriate for candles would be red, black, silver, white, green, blue, and turquoise.

Animals: Baboon, dog, ibis.

Associations: Patron of scribes, physicians, magicians, astronomers, and architects; creation deity; moon god; god of science; god of wisdom, speech, medicine, and time.

Epithets: Lord of the Holy Words; the Divine Physician; Record Keeper of the Gods; Recorder of Divine Judgment; Excellent of Understanding; Lord of the Houses of Life; Master of Stars and Time; Silver Aten; Recorder of Years; Lord of Time.

Offerings: Gemstones such as opal, especially fire opals; herbs such as lavender or valerian; resinous incense such as storax; liquids such as beer or wine; almonds; any writing instruments; feathers.

Spells: Communication, creativity, healing, inspiration, legal matters, magic, peace, power, protection, purification, reconciliation, spirituality, tranquility.

FOUR

Prosperity Spells

All the spells on the following pages are to be performed over a three-day period, so you will need three candles and three incantation papers. Each can be shortened to a single-day spell, or extended into a fourteen-day spell. In chapter 2 I discussed the types of candles used for spells, so you can choose the appropriate size for your purpose. Each spell will provide you with a comprehensive list of ingredients to choose from, any additional items you may need, suggested incense to be used, and deities who may be invoked.

When using the herbs listed for each spell, take a teaspoon of one and mix in a pinch or two of at least two others (more if you are so inclined). You will need enough herb mixture to sprinkle on the altar and on offerings or personal items, but a large quantity is not really needed. The incense I have indicated for each spell is the best choice; however, the following may be used in place of the listed incense for any of the spells: copal, dragon's blood, frankincense, lavender, myrrh, patchouli, sage, or sandalwood. All are easily available and are protective in nature to guard the practitioner during spellwork.

Fortune Increase

Use this spell to attract financial gain, either through the repayment of monies owed you, at job review time for a raise, or whenever participating in games of chance, as in lotteries or casinos.

Fortune Increase Oil:

> 1 teaspoon base oil
> 4 drops allspice essential oil
> 8 drops five-finger grass essential oil
> 4 drops patchouli essential oil

Deities: Geb, Hapy, Khnum, Min, Mut.

Candle: Choose a color related to the deity or deities you will be addressing; or use black, blue, green, orange, white, or yellow, which are appropriate for all of the spells in this book.

Incense: Cinnamon.

Suggested Herbs: Acorn, chicory, lemon verbena, rosemary, yellow dock.

Offering: Coins, dollar bills, lottery tickets.

Incantation Paper Inscription: As this paper burns, may my monetary needs be eased.

Spell Directions

Take a pinch of herbs and sprinkle or blow it onto your altar.

Recite the following invocation:

> Open my mind
> Open my heart
> To all the strength
> That lies within
>
> Do not let fear
> Halt my quest
> Do not let doubt
> Cloud my mind
>
> I have the power
> To bring about change
> I have the ability
> To possess all I desire

Steady my hand
Strengthen my resolve
Allow what I now begin
To reach its natural conclusion

I ask the power of (deity name/the ancients)
Remove all obstacles to my goal
Make my dream reality
Make my wish come true.

Place one incense stick (or cone) in the incense holder, light it, and think about the intent of your spell. If you wish to add your own words, this would be a good point at which to do so. Anoint one of the candles with oil, place it in the candleholder, light it, and recite the following incantation:

I call to the gods for wisdom and guidance
Look favorably upon my request
As I light this candle for attracting money
My intentions are not entirely selfish
I ask only for a good and happy life
I have tried all other avenues
And feel the only way to achieve this
Is by asking for your assistance in attaining my
    goal

> May my request be granted
> May all good things come to pass.

Take a drop of oil and anoint the plate, then lightly rub one of the incantation papers with your oiled fingers. Take the offering, put it on the plate, and position it in front of the candle. Take a pinch of the herbs and sprinkle on the offering. Take the quartz crystal and place it with the herbs and offering on the plate. Put the remaining herbs on the altar. Recite the following spell:

> My needs are great
> Though my request is simple
> All I ask for
> Is enough to be secure
> A good home
> A good living
> A stable career
> A cushion in lean times
> Help me attain my goals.

Take the oiled incantation paper, recite the words on the paper, light it from the candle flame, drop it in the bowl, and finish with the following:

> Now my spell begins
> May my magic find its mark.

Allow the incense and candle to burn out on their own.

Each evening, light one stick (cone) of incense, plus one anointed candle, and recite the spell. Take a dab of oil and lightly touch an incantation paper. Recite the words on the incantation paper, light it from the candle flame, drop it in the bowl, and end with the words:

> My spell has been cast
> May nothing stop its course.

On the final evening, light the last stick (cone) of incense and the last anointed candle, and recite the spell. Dab a bit of oil on the last incantation paper. Recite the words on the incantation paper, light it from the candle flame, drop it in the bowl, and close the spellwork with the following:

> My spell is now complete
> May the result be all I desire.

The following morning, dispose of the candle remnants by throwing them in the trash. The quartz crystal, offering, and paper ash may be kept on the altar with the remaining herb mixture, or you may wish to carry the quartz with you for good luck. If money was used as an offering, use it as a donation, give it to someone in need, or use it to buy a lottery ticket. Passing on the prosperity will bring it back to you in unexpected ways. Spells manifest in many forms, so be patient as the results may not be immediate.

Change of Luck

Use this spell to chase away bad luck. When the spell is complete, take the coin offering and place it in a spell jar filled with honey or molasses on your altar and sprinkle a bit of your herb mixture in as well. Leave the spell bottle on your altar for thirty days, then remove the coin, wash it thoroughly in warm water, and pass it along by spending it.

Change of Luck Oil:

  1 teaspoon base oil
  8 drops clove essential oil
  8 drops dragon's blood essential oil
  8 drops sandalwood essential oil
  1 black peppercorn

Deities: Apophis, Hathor, Horus, Sekhmet, Set.

Candle: Choose a color related to the deity or deities you will be addressing; or use black, blue, green, orange, white, or yellow, which are appropriate for all of the spells in this book.

Incense: Copal.

Suggested Herbs: Angelica, burdock, gentian, lime, raspberry.

Offerings: Coins, dollar bills.

Incantation Paper Inscription: As this paper burns, cast bad luck away from me.

Spell Directions

Take a pinch of herbs and sprinkle or blow it onto your altar.

Recite the following invocation:

> Open my mind
> Open my heart
> To all the strength
> That lies within
>
> Do not let fear
> Halt my quest
> Do not let doubt
> Cloud my mind
>
> I have the power
> To bring about change
> I have the ability
> To possess all I desire
>
> Steady my hand
> Strengthen my resolve
> Allow what I now begin
> To reach its natural conclusion

> I ask the power of (deity name/the ancients)
> Remove all obstacles to my goal
> Make my dream reality
> Make my wish come true.

Place one incense stick (or cone) in the incense holder, light it, and think about the intent of your spell. If you wish to add your own words, this would be a good point at which to do so. Anoint one of the candles with oil, place it in the candleholder, light it, and recite the following incantation:

> I call to the gods for wisdom and guidance
> Look favorably upon my request
> As I light this candle to banish bad luck
> My intentions are not entirely selfish
> I ask only for a good and happy life
> I have tried all other avenues
> And feel the only way to achieve this
> Is by asking for your assistance in attaining my
>   goal
> May my request be granted
> May all good things come to pass.

Take a drop of oil and anoint the plate, then lightly rub one of the incantation papers with your oiled fingers. Take the offering, put it on the plate, and position it in

front of the candle. Take a pinch of the herbs and sprinkle on the offering. Take the quartz crystal and place it with the herbs and offering on the plate. Put the remaining herbs on the altar. Recite the following spell:

> If it wasn't for bad luck
> I'd have no luck at all
> So I need a change
> And not for the worst
> Others have good luck
> They seem to be blessed
> Now it's my time
> To reap the rewards
> Change my luck from bad to good.

Take the oiled incantation paper, recite the words on the paper, light it from the candle flame, drop it into the bowl, and finish with the following:

> Now my spell begins
> May my magic find its mark.

Allow the incense and candle to burn out on their own.

Each evening, light one stick (cone) of incense, plus one anointed candle, and recite the spell. Take a dab of oil and lightly touch an incantation paper. Recite the words on the incantation paper, light it from the candle flame, drop it into the bowl, and end with the words:

My spell has been cast
May nothing stop its course.

On the final evening, light the last stick (cone) of incense and the last anointed candle, and recite the spell. Dab a bit of oil on the last incantation paper. Recite the words on the incantation paper, light it from the candle flame, drop it into the bowl, and close the spellwork with the following:

My spell is now complete
May the result be all I desire.

The following morning, dispose of the candle remnants by throwing them in the trash. The quartz crystal and paper ash may be kept on the altar with the remaining herb mixture, or you may wish to carry the quartz with you for good luck. Take the money offering and use it as a donation, give it to someone in need, or buy a lottery ticket. Passing on the prosperity will bring it back to you in unexpected ways. Spells manifest in many forms, so be patient as the results may not be immediate.

New Venture

Use this spell when starting a new job, career, or business. It is ideally suited for a spell bottle using water, vodka, or wine. Drop a coin and sprinkle a bit of herbs into the liquid; put to one side while you work the spell. When you have completed your work, sprinkle the liquid around the perimeter of your new business or work area for increased success.

New Venture Oil:

    1 teaspoon base oil

    8 drops clove essential oil

    8 drops frankincense essential oil

    8 drops patchouli essential oil

    2 apple seeds

Deities: Bes, Heqet, Isis, Khepri, Sokar.

Candle: Choose a color related to the deity or deities you will be addressing; or use black, blue, green, orange, white, or yellow, which are appropriate for all of the spells in this book.

Incense: Benzoin.

Suggested Herbs: Acacia, carob, ginseng, oak, scullcap.

Offerings: Coins, dollar bills.

Incantation Paper Inscription: As this paper burns, may success begin anew for me.

Spell Directions

Take a pinch of herbs and sprinkle or blow it onto your altar.

Recite the following invocation:

Open my mind
Open my heart
To all the strength
That lies within

Do not let fear
Halt my quest
Do not let doubt
Cloud my mind

I have the power
To bring about change
I have the ability
To possess all I desire

Steady my hand
Strengthen my resolve
Allow what I now begin
To reach its natural conclusion

I ask the power of (deity name/the ancients)
Remove all obstacles to my goal
Make my dream reality
Make my wish come true.

Place one incense stick (or cone) in the incense holder, light it, and think about the intent of your spell. If you wish to add your own words, this would be a good point at which to do so. Anoint one of the candles with oil, place it in the candleholder, light it, and recite the following incantation:

> I call to the gods for wisdom and guidance
> Look favorably upon my request
> As I light this candle for a new beginning
> My intentions are not entirely selfish
> I ask only for a good and happy life
> I have tried all other avenues
> And feel the only way to achieve this
> Is by asking for your assistance in attaining my
>   goal
> May my request be granted
> May all good things come to pass.

Take a drop of oil and anoint the plate, then lightly rub one of the incantation papers with your oiled fingers. Take the offering, put it on the plate, and position it in front of the candle. Take a pinch of the herbs and sprinkle on the offering. Take the quartz crystal and place it with the herbs and offering on the plate. Put the remaining herbs on the altar. Recite the following spell:

> I stand at the brink
> Of a brand new path

> Anticipation
> Excitement
> And trepidation
> Fill my mind and heart
> Help me take my first step
> Into the unknown void
> May my choice be a wise one.

Take the oiled incantation paper, recite the words on the paper, light it from the candle flame, drop it in the bowl, and finish with the following:

> Now my spell begins
> May my magic find its mark.

Allow the incense and candle to burn out on their own.

Each evening, light one stick (cone) of incense, plus one anointed candle, and recite the spell. Take a dab of oil and lightly touch an incantation paper. Recite the words on the incantation paper, light it from the candle flame, drop it in the bowl, and end with the words:

> My spell has been cast
> May nothing stop its course.

On the final evening, light the last stick (cone) of incense and the last anointed candle, and recite the spell. Dab a bit of oil on the last incantation paper. Recite the words on the incantation paper, light it from the candle flame, drop it in the bowl, and close the spellwork with the following:

> My spell is now complete
> May the results be all I desire.

The following morning, dispose of the candle remnants by throwing them in the trash. The quartz crystal and paper ash may be kept on the altar with the remaining herb mixture, or you may wish to carry the quartz with you for good luck. As noted above, use the liquid for attracting the prosperity needed. Take the money offering from the altar and spend it on the new venture. Passing on the prosperity will bring it back to you in unexpected ways. Spells manifest in many forms, so be patient as the results may not be immediate.

Blessed Success

This is a spell to bless your path as you search for success. You may find this spell will lead to several offers of employment or may open up avenues you never considered before.

Blessed Success Oil:

    1 teaspoon base oil
    6 drops anise essential oil

8 drops carnation essential oil
6 drops geranium essential oil
pinch of flax seeds

Deities: Amun, Bes, Horus, Isis, Min.

Candle: Choose a color related to the deity or deities you will be addressing; or use black, blue, green, orange, white, or yellow, which are appropriate for all of the spells in this book.

Incense: Holly.

Suggested Herbs: Almond, cardamom, eucalyptus, lady's mantle, parsley.

Offerings: Coins, dollar bills.

Incantation Paper Inscription: As this paper burns, may blessings rain down upon me.

Spell Directions

Take a pinch of herbs and sprinkle or blow it onto your altar.

Recite the following invocation:

> Open my mind
> Open my heart
> To all the strength
> That lies within
>
> Do not let fear
> Halt my quest

Do not let doubt
Cloud my mind

I have the power
To bring about change
I have the ability
To possess all I desire

Steady my hand
Strengthen my resolve
Allow what I now begin
To reach its natural conclusion

I ask the power of (deity name/the ancients)
Remove all obstacles to my goal
Make my dream reality
Make my wish come true.

Place one incense stick (or cone) in the incense holder, light it, and think about the intent of your spell. If you wish to add your own words, this would be a good point at which to do so. Anoint one of the candles with oil, place it in the candleholder, light it, and recite the following incantation:

I call to the gods for wisdom and guidance
Look favorably upon my request
As I light this candle for blessings

My intentions are not entirely selfish
I ask only for a good and happy life
I have tried all other avenues
And feel the only way to achieve this
Is by asking for your assistance in attaining my
    goal
May my request be granted
May all good things come to pass.

Take a drop of oil and anoint the plate, then lightly rub one of the incantation papers with your oiled fingers. Take the offering, put it on the plate, and position it in front of the candle. Take a pinch of the herbs and sprinkle on the offering. Take the quartz crystal and place it with the herbs and offering on the plate. Put the remaining herbs on the altar. Recite the following spell:

Bless this path
I choose to take
The path to my success
It may be fraught
With peril and doubt
But I shall see it through
And at the end
My joy will be
The career I hope to find.

Take the oiled incantation paper, recite the words on the paper, light it from the candle flame, drop it in the bowl, and finish with the following:

> Now my spell begins
> May my magic find its mark.

Allow the incense and candle to burn out on their own.

Each evening, light one stick (cone) of incense, plus one anointed candle, and recite the spell. Take a dab of oil and lightly touch an incantation paper. Recite the words on the incantation paper, light it from the candle flame, drop it in the bowl, and end with the words:

> My spell has been cast
> May nothing stop its course.

On the final evening, light the last stick (cone) of incense and the last anointed candle, and recite the spell. Dab a bit of oil on the last incantation paper. Recite the words on the incantation paper, light it from the candle flame, drop it in the bowl, and close the spellwork with the following:

> My spell is now complete
> May the results be all I desire.

The following morning, dispose of the candle remnants by throwing them in the trash. The quartz crystal, offering, and paper ash may be kept on the altar with the remaining herb mixture, or you may wish to carry the quartz with you for good luck. Take the money offering and use it as a donation, give it to someone in need, or buy a lottery ticket. Passing on the prosperity will bring it back to you in unexpected ways. Spells manifest in many forms, so be patient as the results may not be immediate.

I'm the Best

Let prospective employers see you shine. This spell will help your résumé stand out above others and will make you shine at interviews. If you use a résumé for your offering, place it to one side on your altar, sprinkle with a little herb mixture, and take care not to get oil or candle wax on it. If you use a coin offering, you can drop it into a liquid (water, vodka, or wine with herbs) until the day of the interview, and sprinkle some of the liquid outside the building where the interview takes place.

I'm the Best Oil:

1 teaspoon base oil
6 drops allspice essential oil
8 drops frankincense essential oil

6 drops rose essential oil

Deities: Bes, Hathor, Isis, Osiris, Thoth.

Candle: Choose a color related to the deity or deities you will be addressing; or use black, blue, green, orange, white, or yellow, which are appropriate for all of the spells in this book.

Incense: Gardenia.

Suggested Herbs: Aspen, balm of gilead, coltsfoot, hibiscus, pansy.

Offerings: Coins, dollar bills, résumé, business card.

Incantation Paper Inscription: As this paper burns, make me shine above the rest.

Spell Directions

Take a pinch of herbs and sprinkle or blow it onto your altar.

Recite the following invocation:

> Open my mind
> Open my heart
> To all the strength
> That lies within
>
> Do not let fear
> Halt my quest
> Do not let doubt
> Cloud my mind

I have the power
To bring about change
I have the ability
To possess all I desire

Steady my hand
Strengthen my resolve
Allow what I now begin
To reach its natural conclusion

I ask the power of (deity name/the ancients)
Remove all obstacles to my goal
Make my dream reality
Make my wish come true.

Place one incense stick (or cone) in the incense holder, light it, and think about the intent of your spell. If you wish to add your own words, this would be a good point at which to do so. Anoint one of the candles with oil, place it in the candleholder, light it, and recite the following incantation:

I call to the gods for wisdom and guidance
Look favorably upon my request
As I light this candle to shout my worth
My intentions are not entirely selfish
I ask only for a good and happy life
I have tried all other avenues

And feel the only way to achieve this
Is by asking for your assistance in attaining my
   goal
May my request be granted
May all good things come to pass.

Take a drop of oil and anoint the plate, then lightly rub one of the incantation papers with your oiled fingers. Take the offering, put it on the plate (or on the altar), and position it in front of the candle. Take a pinch of the herbs and sprinkle on the offering. Take the quartz crystal and place it with the herbs and offering on the plate. Put the remaining herbs on the altar. Recite the following spell:

I have many talents
I'm the best I can be
See my potential
Look past my shortcomings
I'll do a great job
I'll work hard
And shine brightly
For I have many talents
I'm the best you will find.

Take the oiled incantation paper, recite the words on the paper, light it from the candle flame, drop it into the bowl, and finish with the following:

> Now my spell begins
> May my magic find its mark.

Allow the incense and candle to burn out on their own.

Each evening, light one stick (cone) of incense, plus one anointed candle, and recite the spell. Take a dab of oil and lightly touch an incantation paper. Recite the words on the incantation paper, light it from the candle flame, drop it into the bowl, and end with the words:

> My spell has been cast
> May nothing stop its course.

On the final evening, light the last stick (cone) of incense and the last anointed candle, and recite the spell. Dab a bit of oil on the last incantation paper. Recite the words on the incantation paper, light it from the candle flame, drop it into the bowl, and close the spellwork with the following:

> My spell is now complete
> May the result be all I desire.

The following morning, dispose of the candle remnants by throwing them in the trash. The quartz crystal, offering, and paper ash may be kept on the altar with the remaining herb mixture, or you may wish to carry the quartz with you for good luck. If money was used as an offering, use it as a donation, give it to someone in need, or buy a lottery ticket. Passing on the prosperity will bring it back to you in unexpected ways. If your offering was a résumé, send it out to a prospective employer and wait to see the results. Spells manifest in many forms, so be patient as the results may not be immediate.

Create My Success

This is a good spell for those looking for success in the arts. It will help to stir creativity and overcome any type of creative slump.

Create My Success Oil:

    1 teaspoon base oil

    4 drops benzoin essential oil

    8 drops cinnamon essential oil

    8 drops vanilla essential oil

Deities: Isis, Khnum, Osiris, Ptah, Thoth.

Candle: Choose a color related to the deity or deities you will be addressing; or use black, blue, green, orange, white, or yellow, which are appropriate for all of the spells in this book.

Incense: Lotus.

Suggested Herbs: Apple, barley, catnip, grape, maple.

Offerings: Coins, items used in creative ventures such as a paintbrush, pen, guitar pick, etc.

Incantation Paper Inscription: As this paper burns, so too shall creativity burn within me.

Spell Directions

Take a pinch of herbs and sprinkle or blow it onto your altar.

Recite the following invocation:

> Open my mind
> Open my heart
> To all the strength
> That lies within
>
> Do not let fear
> Halt my quest
> Do not let doubt
> Cloud my mind
>
> I have the power
> To bring about change
> I have the ability
> To possess all I desire

Steady my hand
Strengthen my resolve
Allow what I now begin
To reach its natural conclusion

I ask the power of (deity name/the ancients)
Remove all obstacles to my goal
Make my dream reality
Make my wish come true.

Place one incense stick (or cone) in the incense holder, light it, and think about the intent of your spell. If you wish to add your own words, this would be a good point at which to do so. Anoint one of the candles with oil, place it in the candleholder, light it, and recite the following incantation:

I call to the gods for wisdom and guidance
Look favorably upon my request
As I light this candle for creativity
My intentions are not entirely selfish
I ask only for a good and happy life
I have tried all other avenues
And feel the only way to achieve this
Is by asking for your assistance in attaining my
    goal
May my request be granted

May all good things come to pass.

Take a drop of oil and anoint the plate, then lightly rub one of the incantation papers with your oiled fingers. Take the offering, put it on the plate (if it does not fit, place it on the altar), and position it in front of the candle. Take a pinch of the herbs and sprinkle on the offering. Take the quartz crystal and place it with the herbs and offering on the plate. Put the remaining herbs on the altar. Recite the following spell:

> Spark the fire of ideas
> Let them flow freely
> Help me express myself
> Through pen and paper
> Paint and canvas
> Any method will do
> Bring my ideas to light
> Make them tangible
> Make them unique.

Take the oiled incantation paper, recite the words on the paper, light it from the candle flame, drop it in the bowl, and finish with the following:

> Now my spell begins
> May my magic find its mark.

Allow the incense and candle to burn out on their own.

Each evening, light one stick (cone) of incense, plus one anointed candle, and recite the spell. Take a dab of oil and lightly touch an incantation paper. Recite the words on the incantation paper, light it from the candle flame, drop it in the bowl, and end with the words:

> My spell has been cast
> May nothing stop its course.

On the final evening, light the last stick (cone) of incense and the last anointed candle, and recite the spell. Dab a bit of oil on the last incantation paper. Recite the words on the incantation paper, light it from the candle flame, drop it in the bowl, and close the spellwork with the following:

> My spell is now complete
> May the result be all I desire.

The following morning, dispose of the candle remnants by throwing them in the trash. The quartz crystal, offering, and paper ash may be kept on the altar with the remaining herb mixture, or you may wish to carry the quartz with you for good luck. If you included a creative item as your offering, use it in your next endeavor. If money was included, use it as a donation, give it to someone in need, or use it to buy creative supplies. Passing on the prosperity will bring it back to you in unexpected ways. Spells manifest in many forms, so be patient as the results may not be immediate.

Road Be Clear

Use this spell to clear negativity from any job searches, interviews, career changes, or ventures of any kind. Sometimes bad feelings linger after a job change, and sometimes we inadvertently derail our own attempts to get ahead. You want to get rid of that type of energy so you can move forward in a positive direction.

Road Be Clear Oil:
    1 teaspoon base oil
    6 drops anise essential oil
    8 drops lemon essential oil
    8 drops myrrh essential oil

Deities: Apophis, Hathor, Horus, Sekhmet, Sobek.

Candle: Choose a color related to the deity or deities you will be addressing; or use black, blue, green, orange, white, or yellow, which are appropriate for all of the spells in this book.

Incense: Fir.

Suggested Herbs: Agrimony, black pepper, eyebright, horehound, nettle.

Offerings: Coins, dollar bills.

Incantation Paper Inscription: As this paper burns, cast aside all negative energy.

Spell Directions

Take a pinch of herbs and sprinkle or blow it onto your altar.

Recite the following invocation:

> Open my mind
> Open my heart
> To all the strength
> That lies within
>
> Do not let fear
> Halt my quest
> Do not let doubt
> Cloud my mind
>
> I have the power
> To bring about change
> I have the ability
> To possess all I desire
>
> Steady my hand
> Strengthen my resolve
> Allow what I now begin
> To reach its natural conclusion

I ask the power of (deity name/the ancients)
Remove all obstacles to my goal
Make my dream reality
Make my wish come true.

Place one incense stick (or cone) in the incense holder, light it, and think about the intent of your spell. If you wish to add your own words, this would be a good point at which to do so. Anoint one of the candles with oil, place it in the candleholder, light it, and recite the following incantation:

I call to the gods for wisdom and guidance
Look favorably upon my request
As I light this candle to dispel negativity
My intentions are not entirely selfish
I ask only for a good and happy life
I have tried all other avenues
And feel the only way to achieve this
Is by asking for your assistance in attaining my
    goal
May my request be granted
May all good things come to pass.

Take a drop of oil and anoint the plate, then lightly rub one of the incantation papers with your oiled fingers. Take the offering, put it on the plate, and position it in

front of the candle. Take a pinch of the herbs and sprinkle on the offering. Take the quartz crystal and place it with the herbs and offering on the plate. Put the remaining herbs on the altar. Recite the following spell:

> Ill will surrounds me
> Causing pain and hardship
> Make the evil forces
> Dissipate and scatter
> Turn the bad to good
> Make the difficult easy
> Help remove the blocks
> Which have been set in my path
> So I may achieve all I can.

Take the oiled incantation paper, recite the words on the paper, light it from the candle flame, drop it into the bowl, and finish with the following:

> Now my spell begins
> May my magic find its mark.

Allow the incense and candle to burn out on their own.

Each evening, light one stick (cone) of incense, plus one anointed candle, and recite the spell. Take a dab of oil and lightly touch an incantation paper. Recite the

words on the incantation paper, light it from the candle flame, drop it into the bowl, and end with the words:

> My spell has been cast
> May nothing stop its course.

On the final evening, light the last stick (cone) of incense and the last anointed candle, and recite the spell. Dab a bit of oil on the last incantation paper. Recite the words on the incantation paper, light it from the candle flame, drop it into the bowl, and close the spellwork with the following:

> My spell is now complete
> May the result be all I desire.

The following morning, dispose of the candle remnants by throwing them in the trash. The quartz crystal, offering, and paper ash may be kept on the altar with the remaining herb mixture, or you may wish to carry the quartz with you for good luck. Take the money offering and use it as a donation, give it to someone in need, or buy a lottery ticket. Passing on the prosperity will bring it back to you in unexpected ways. Spells manifest in many forms, so be patient as the results may not be immediate.

Undeserved

This is a useful spell for anyone who has experienced a job change of any kind, such as a job loss, layoff, transfer, or restructuring, which was not of one's choosing. When the spell is complete, take the coin offering and place it in a spell jar filled with honey to sweeten up your job outlook and sprinkle a bit of herbs in as well. Keep the spell bottle on your altar for thirty days, then remove the coin, wash thoroughly, and pass it along.

Undeserved Oil:

1 teaspoon base oil

6 drops clove essential oil

8 drops myrrh essential oil

4 drops orris essential oil

2-4 small sunflower seeds

Deities: Apophis, Khepri, Osiris, Sekhmet, Sokar.

Candle: Choose a color related to the deity or deities you will be addressing; or use black, blue, green, orange, white, or yellow, which are appropriate for all of the spells in this book.

Incense: Heliotrope.

Suggested Herbs: Anemone, cayenne pepper, elm, lily, southernwood.

Offerings: Coins, dollar bills.

Incantation Paper Inscription: As this paper burns, close this chapter of my life.

Spell Directions

Take a pinch of herbs and sprinkle or blow it onto your altar.

Recite the following invocation:

> Open my mind
> Open my heart
> To all the strength
> That lies within
>
> Do not let fear
> Halt my quest
> Do not let doubt
> Cloud my mind
>
> I have the power
> To bring about change
> I have the ability
> To possess all I desire
>
> Steady my hand
> Strengthen my resolve
> Allow what I now begin
> To reach its natural conclusion

> I ask the power of (deity name/the ancients)
> Remove all obstacles to my goal
> Make my dream reality
> Make my wish come true.

Place one incense stick (or cone) in the incense holder, light it, and think about the intent of your spell. If you wish to add your own words, this would be a good point at which to do so. Anoint one of the candles with oil, place it in the candleholder, light it, and recite the following incantation:

> I call to the gods for wisdom and guidance
> Look favorably upon my request
> As I light this candle for endings
> My intentions are not entirely selfish
> I ask only for a good and happy life
> I have tried all other avenues
> And feel the only way to achieve this
> Is by asking for your assistance in attaining my
>   goal
> May my request be granted
> May all good things come to pass.

Take a drop of oil and anoint the plate, then lightly rub one of the incantation papers with your oiled fingers. Take the offering, put it on the plate, and position it in

front of the candle. Take a pinch of the herbs and sprinkle on the offering. Take the quartz crystal and place it with the herbs and offering on the plate. Put the remaining herbs on the altar. Recite the following spell:

> My ordered existence
> Is in a state of disorder
> My solid foundation
> Has crumbled beneath my feet
> I know I will recover
> And find something better for me
> Look to the future
> For this (layoff/job loss/transfer) was unseen
> And I deserve so much more.

Take the oiled incantation paper, recite the words on the paper, light it from the candle flame, drop it in the bowl, and finish with the following:

> Now my spell begins
> May my magic find its mark.

Allow the incense and candle to burn out on their own.

Each evening, light one stick (cone) of incense, plus one anointed candle, and recite the spell. Take a dab of oil and lightly touch an incantation paper. Recite the words on the incantation paper, light it from the candle flame, drop it in the bowl, and end with the words:

> My spell has been cast
> May nothing stop its course.

On the final evening, light the last stick (cone) of incense and the last anointed candle, and recite the spell. Dab a bit of oil on the last incantation paper. Recite the words on the incantation paper, light it from the candle flame, drop it in the bowl, and close the spellwork with the following:

> My spell is now complete
> May the result be all I desire.

The following morning, dispose of the candle remnants by throwing them in the trash. The quartz crystal, offering, and paper ash may be kept on the altar with the remaining herb mixture, or you may wish to carry the quartz with you for good luck. Take the money offering and use it as a donation, give it to someone in need, or buy a lottery ticket. Passing on the prosperity will bring it back to you in unexpected ways. Spells manifest in many forms, so be patient as the results may not be immediate.

Success Can Be Mine

Use this spell to find new paths to success in creative endeavors. This is a great spell for those creative people who find themselves with a block of some kind; it can help open up the gates of inspiration.

Success Can Be Mine Oil:

    1 teaspoon base oil
    8 drops benzoin essential oil
    8 drops five-finger grass essential oil
    4 drops honeysuckle essential oil

Deities: Amun, Imhotep, Isis, Osiris, Seshat.

Candle: Choose a color related to the deity or deities you will be addressing; or use black, blue, green, orange, white, or yellow, which are appropriate for all of the spells in this book.

Incense: Jasmine.

Suggested Herbs: Arrowroot, birch, damiana, hops, lemongrass.

Offerings: Coins, items used in creative ventures such as a paintbrush, pen, guitar pick, etc.

Incantation Paper Inscription: As this paper burns, ignite the spark of inspiration within me.

Spell Directions

Take a pinch of herbs and sprinkle or blow it onto your altar.

Recite the following invocation:

> Open my mind
> Open my heart
> To all the strength
> That lies within
>
> Do not let fear
> Halt my quest
> Do not let doubt
> Cloud my mind
>
> I have the power
> To bring about change
> I have the ability
> To possess all I desire
>
> Steady my hand
> Strengthen my resolve
> Allow what I now begin
> To reach its natural conclusion
>
> I ask the power of (deity name/the ancients)
> Remove all obstacles to my goal
> Make my dream reality
> Make my wish come true.

Place one incense stick (or cone) in the incense holder, light it, and think about the intent of your spell. If you wish to add your own words, this would be a good point at which to do so. Anoint one of the candles with oil, place it in the candleholder, light it, and recite the following incantation:

> I call to the gods for wisdom and guidance
> Look favorably upon my request
> As I light this candle for inspiration
> My intentions are not entirely selfish
> I ask only for a good and happy life
> I have tried all other avenues
> And feel the only way to achieve this
> Is by asking for your assistance in attaining my
>   goal
> May my request be granted
> May all good things come to pass.

Take a drop of oil and anoint the plate, then lightly rub one of the incantation papers with your oiled fingers. Take the offering, put it on the plate (or place it on the altar if it's too large), and position it in front of the candle. Take a pinch of the herbs and sprinkle on the offering. Take the quartz crystal and place it with the herbs and item on the plate. Put the remaining herbs on the altar. Recite the following spell:

> A cold dark mist
> Clouds my thoughts
> Lift the veil
> That blocks my view
> Light the flame
> Make it burn brightly
> Illuminate my imagination
> So it can flow freely
> And shine for all to see.

Take the oiled incantation paper, recite the words on the paper, light it from the candle flame, drop it in the bowl, and finish with the following:

> Now my spell begins
> May my magic find its mark.

Allow the incense and candle to burn out on their own.

Each evening, light one stick (cone) of incense, plus one anointed candle, and recite the spell. Take a dab of oil and lightly touch an incantation paper. Recite the words on the incantation paper, light it from the candle flame, drop it in the bowl, and end with the words:

> My spell has been cast
> May nothing stop its course.

On the final evening, light the last stick (cone) of incense and the last anointed candle, and recite the spell. Dab a bit of oil on the last incantation paper. Recite the words on the incantation paper, light it from the candle flame, drop it in the bowl, and close the spellwork with the following:

> My spell is now complete
> May the result be all I desire.

The following morning, dispose of the candle remnants by throwing them in the trash. The quartz crystal, offering, and paper ash may be kept on the altar with the remaining herb mixture, or you may wish to carry the quartz with you for good luck. If you included a creative item as your offering, use it in your next endeavor. If money was included, use it as a donation, give it to someone in need, or use it to buy creative supplies. Passing on the prosperity will bring it back to you in unexpected ways. Spells manifest in many forms, so be patient as the results may not be immediate.

Find the Right Career

Use this spell when starting the job search and interview cycle. Take one coin, drop it in a spell bottle of liquid (such as water, vodka, or wine), sprinkle in herbs, and place it on your altar during the spellwork. When the spell is concluded, sprinkle the liquid outside a prospective employer's business, rub some on your hands before an interview, or add a little to your bath water. Be creative!

Find the Right Career Oil:
>   1 teaspoon base oil
>   4 drops cinnamon essential oil
>   10 drops five-finger grass essential oil
>   8 drops orange essential oil

Deities: Bes, Horus, Isis, Khnum, Mut.

Candle: Choose a color related to the deity or deities you will be addressing; or use black, blue, green, orange, white, or yellow, which are appropriate for all of the spells in this book.

Incense: Orange.

Suggested Herbs: Bay, caraway, echinacea, Irish moss, lovage.

Offerings: Coins, résumés, business cards, job listings.

Incantation Paper Inscription: As this paper burns, make the job market sizzle for me.

Spell Directions

Take a pinch of herbs and sprinkle or blow it onto your altar.

Recite the following invocation:

> Open my mind
> Open my heart
> To all the strength
> That lies within
>
> Do not let fear
> Halt my quest
> Do not let doubt
> Cloud my mind
>
> I have the power
> To bring about change
> I have the ability
> To possess all I desire
>
> Steady my hand
> Strengthen my resolve
> Allow what I now begin
> To reach its natural conclusion

> I ask the power of (deity name/the ancients)
> Remove all obstacles to my goal
> Make my dream reality
> Make my wish come true.

Place one incense stick (or cone) in the incense holder, light it, and think about the intent of your spell. If you wish to add your own words, this would be a good point at which to do so. Anoint one of the candles with oil, place it in the candleholder, light it, and recite the following incantation:

> I call to the gods for wisdom and guidance
> Look favorably upon my request
> As I light this candle for career choices
> My intentions are not entirely selfish
> I ask only for a good and happy life
> I have tried all other avenues
> And feel the only way to achieve this
> Is by asking for your assistance in attaining my
>   goal
> May my request be granted
> May all good things come to pass.

Take a drop of oil and anoint the plate, then lightly rub one of the incantation papers with your oiled fingers. Take the offering, put it on the plate or next to it, and position it in front of the candle. Take a pinch of the herbs and sprinkle on the offering. Take the quartz crystal and place it with the herbs and offering on the plate. Put the remaining herbs on the altar. Recite the following spell:

> Open up pathways
> I have never considered
> Make me attractive
> To all I encounter
> Let my talents shine
> As bright as the sun
> Help make my search
> A short but profitable one
> I am worthy of the best life has to offer.

Take the oiled incantation paper, recite the words on the paper, light it from the candle flame, drop it in the bowl, and finish with the following:

> Now my spell begins
> May my magic find its mark.

Allow the incense and candle to burn out on their own.

Each evening, light one stick (cone) of incense, plus one anointed candle, and recite the spell. Take a dab of oil and lightly touch an incantation paper. Recite the

words on the incantation paper, light it from the candle flame, drop it in the bowl, and end with the words:

> My spell has been cast
> May nothing stop its course.

On the final evening, light the last stick (cone) of incense and the last anointed candle, and recite the spell. Dab a bit of oil on the last incantation paper. Recite the words on the incantation paper, light it from the candle flame, drop it in the bowl, and close the spellwork with the following:

> My spell is now complete
> May the result be all I desire.

The following morning, dispose of the candle remnants by throwing them in the trash. The quartz crystal, offering, and paper ash may be kept on the altar with the remaining herb mixture, or you may wish to carry the quartz with you for good luck. If the offering was a coin, use it as a donation, give it to someone in need, or buy a lottery ticket. Passing on the prosperity will bring it back to you in unexpected ways. If the offering was a résumé, use it for the job you most want. Keep the business cards and/or job listings on the altar to attract prospective employers. Spells manifest in many forms, so be patient as the results may not be immediate.

Invincible

This spell helps overcome anything; you want nothing to stand in the way of your success. Place one coin in a spell bottle of liquid (such as water, vodka, or wine), sprinkle in herbs, and put it on your altar during the spellwork. At the conclusion of the spell, spend the coin and pass the prosperity around, and sprinkle the liquid around your house, place of business, or wherever it will do the most good for your success. Additionally, if you are looking for financing for a startup business, you could sprinkle the liquid outside the bank before your meeting.

Invincible Oil:

    1 teaspoon base oil
    8 drops allspice essential oil
    4 drops honeysuckle essential oil
    8 drops musk essential oil

Deities: Horus, Montu, Sekhmet, Set, Sobek.

Candle: Choose a color related to the deity or deities you will be addressing; or use black, blue, green, orange, white, or yellow, which are appropriate for all of the spells in this book.

Incense: Cedar.

Suggested Herbs: Black cohosh, centaury, dodder, primrose, thistle.

Offerings: Coins, dollar bills.

Incantation Paper Inscription: As this paper burns, dissolve all obstacles to my success.

Spell Directions

Take a pinch of herbs and sprinkle or blow it onto your altar.

Recite the following invocation:

> Open my mind
> Open my heart
> To all the strength
> That lies within
>
> Do not let fear
> Halt my quest
> Do not let doubt
> Cloud my mind
>
> I have the power
> To bring about change
> I have the ability
> To possess all I desire
>
> Steady my hand
> Strengthen my resolve

Allow what I now begin
To reach its natural conclusion

I ask the power of (deity name/the ancients)
Remove all obstacles to my goal
Make my dream reality
Make my wish come true.

Place one incense stick (or cone) in the incense holder, light it, and think about the intent of your spell. If you wish to add your own words, this would be a good point at which to do so. Anoint one of the candles with oil, place it in the candleholder, light it, and recite the following incantation:

I call to the gods for wisdom and guidance
Look favorably upon my request
As I light this candle for overcoming obstacles
My intentions are not entirely selfish
I ask only for a good and happy life
I have tried all other avenues
And feel the only way to achieve this
Is by asking for your assistance in attaining my
    goal
May my request be granted
May all good things come to pass.

Take a drop of oil and anoint the plate, then lightly rub one of the incantation papers with your oiled fingers. Take the offering, put it on the plate, and position it in front of the candle. Take a pinch of the herbs and sprinkle on the offering. Take the quartz crystal and place it with the herbs and offering on the plate. Put the remaining herbs on the altar. Recite the following spell:

> Nothing can stop me
> From attaining my goal
> I have the power
> To conquer anything
> No problem is unsolvable
> No mountain unassailable
> I create my own path
> My destiny is in my hands
> Because nothing can stop me.

Take the oiled incantation paper, recite the words on the paper, light it from the candle flame, drop it in the bowl, and finish with the following:

> Now my spell begins
> May my magic find its mark.

Allow the incense and candle to burn out on their own.

Each evening, light one stick (cone) of incense, plus one anointed candle, and recite the spell. Take a dab of oil and lightly touch an incantation paper. Recite the words on the incantation paper, light it from the candle flame, drop it in the bowl, and end with the words:

> My spell has been cast
> May nothing stop its course.

On the final evening, light the last stick (cone) of incense and the last anointed candle, and recite the spell. Dab a bit of oil on the last incantation paper. Recite the words on the incantation paper, light it from the candle flame, drop it in the bowl, and close the spellwork with the following:

> My spell is now complete
> May the result be all I desire.

The following morning, dispose of the candle remnants by throwing them in the trash. The quartz crystal, offering, and paper ash may be kept on the altar with the remaining herb mixture, or you may wish to carry the quartz with you for good luck. Take the money offering and use it as a donation, give it to someone in need, or buy a lottery ticket. Passing on the prosperity will bring it back to you in unexpected ways. Spells manifest in many forms, so be patient as the results may not be immediate.

Feel the Success

Use this spell like a pat on the back. You know you have the ability to succeed at anything, but sometimes we falter and feel we can't do it. You *can* and this spell will help focus your mind on success and how to achieve it. Take a coin and put it in a spell bottle of liquid (such as water, vodka, or wine), sprinkle in herbs, and keep it on your altar during the spellwork. When you have completed the spell, sprinkle the liquid around your home, office, or wherever your success takes you.

Feel the Success Oil:

    1 teaspoon base oil

    10 drops allspice essential oil

    6 drops dragon's blood essential oil

    6 drops vetivert essential oil

Deities: Amun, Montu, Ptah, Renenutet, Sekhmet.

Candle: Choose a color related to the deity or deities you will be addressing; or use black, blue, green, orange, white, or yellow, which are appropriate for all of the spells in this book.

Incense: Dragon's blood.

Suggested Herbs: Borage, celandine, fennel, licorice, poplar.

Offerings: Coins, dollar bills.

Incantation Paper Inscription: As this paper burns, all things become possible for me to achieve.

Spell Directions

Take a pinch of herbs and sprinkle or blow it onto your altar.

Recite the following invocation:

> Open my mind
> Open my heart
> To all the strength
> That lies within
>
> Do not let fear
> Halt my quest
> Do not let doubt
> Cloud my mind
>
> I have the power
> To bring about change
> I have the ability
> To possess all I desire
>
> Steady my hand
> Strengthen my resolve
> Allow what I now begin
> To reach its natural conclusion

> I ask the power of (deity name/the ancients)
> Remove all obstacles to my goal
> Make my dream reality
> Make my wish come true.

Place one incense stick (or cone) in the incense holder, light it, and think about the intent of your spell. If you wish to add your own words, this would be a good point at which to do so. Anoint one of the candles with oil, place it in the candleholder, light it, and recite the following incantation:

> I call to the gods for wisdom and guidance
> Look favorably upon my request
> As I light this candle for the power to succeed
> My intentions are not entirely selfish
> I ask only for a good and happy life
> I have tried all other avenues
> And feel the only way to achieve this
> Is by asking for your assistance in attaining my
>   goal
> May my request be granted
> May all good things come to pass.

Take a drop of oil and anoint the plate, then lightly rub one of the incantation papers with your oiled fingers. Take the offering, put it on the plate, and position it in

front of the candle. Take a pinch of the herbs and sprinkle on the offering. Take the quartz crystal and place it with the herbs and offering on the plate. Put the remaining herbs on the altar. Recite the following spell:

> Power takes many forms
> To overcome adversity
> To accumulate wealth
> To hold sway over others
> Power aids success
> But power can corrupt
> Help me to know
> When to use my power
> And not to abuse it.

Take the oiled incantation paper, recite the words on the paper, light it from the candle flame, drop it in the bowl, and finish with the following:

> Now my spell begins
> May my magic find its mark.

Allow the incense and candle to burn out on their own.

Each evening, light one stick (cone) of incense, plus one anointed candle, and recite the spell. Take a dab of oil and lightly touch an incantation paper. Recite the words on the incantation paper, light it from the candle flame, drop it in the bowl, and end with the words:

My spell has been cast
May nothing stop its course.

On the final evening, light the last stick (cone) of incense and the last anointed candle, and recite the spell. Dab a bit of oil on the last incantation paper. Recite the words on the incantation paper, light it from the candle flame, drop it in the bowl, and close the spellwork with the following:

My spell is now complete
May the result be all I desire.

The following morning, dispose of the candle remnants by throwing them in the trash. The quartz crystal, offering, and paper ash may be kept on the altar with the remaining herb mixture, or you may wish to carry the quartz with you for good luck. Take the money offering and use it as a donation, give it to someone in need, or buy a lottery ticket. Passing on the prosperity will bring it back to you in unexpected ways. Spells manifest in many forms, so be patient as the results may not be immediate.

On Top of the World

Use this spell to increase prosperity and to enjoy the fruits of your prosperity. Before you start the spell, fill a bottle with honey or molasses. Drop in a coin, sprinkle with herbs, and leave on the altar during the spell.

On Top of the World Oil:
    1 teaspoon base oil
    8 drops clove essential oil
    8 drops five-finger grass essential oil
    8 drops patchouli essential oil

Deities: Geb, Hapy, Min, Mut, Renenutet.

Candle: Choose a color related to the deity or deities you will be addressing; or use black, blue, green, orange, white, or yellow, which are appropriate for all of the spells in this book.

Incense: Patchouli.

Suggested Herbs: Clove, coconut, fenugreek, oat, pecan.

Offerings: Coins, dollar bills.

Incantation Paper Inscription: As this paper burns, may bounty and increase occur.

Spell Directions
Take a pinch of herbs and sprinkle or blow it onto your altar.

Recite the following invocation:

> Open my mind
> Open my heart

To all the strength
That lies within

Do not let fear
Halt my quest
Do not let doubt
Cloud my mind

I have the power
To bring about change
I have the ability
To possess all I desire

Steady my hand
Strengthen my resolve
Allow what I now begin
To reach its natural conclusion

I ask the power of (deity name/the ancients)
Remove all obstacles to my goal
Make my dream reality
Make my wish come true.

Place one incense stick (or cone) in the incense holder, light it, and think about the intent of your spell. If you wish to add your own words, this would be a good point at which to do so. Anoint one of the candles with oil, place it in the candleholder, light it, and recite the following incantation:

> I call to the gods for wisdom and guidance
> Look favorably upon my request
> As I light this candle for prosperity
> My intentions are not entirely selfish
> I ask only for a good and happy life
> I have tried all other avenues
> And feel the only way to achieve this
> Is by asking for your assistance in attaining my
>   goal
> May my request be granted
> May all good things come to pass.

Take a drop of oil and anoint the plate, then lightly rub one of the incantation papers with your oiled fingers. Take the offering, put it on the plate, and position it in front of the candle. Take a pinch of the herbs and sprinkle on the offering. Take the quartz crystal and place it with the herbs and offering on the plate. Put the remaining herbs on the altar until your work is complete. Recite the following spell:

> Make me prosper
> Make me grow
> Give me the tools

> To make my life easier
> Increase my earnings
> Lighten my burden
> Give me the time
> To enjoy my life
> And all I have accomplished.

Take the oiled incantation paper, recite the words on the paper, light it from the candle flame, drop it into the bowl, and finish with the following:

> Now my spell begins
> May my magic find its mark.

Allow the incense and candle to burn out on their own.

Each evening, light one stick (cone) of incense, plus one anointed candle, and recite the spell. Take a dab of oil and lightly touch an incantation paper. Recite the words on the incantation paper, light it from the candle flame, drop it into the bowl, and end with the words:

> My spell has been cast
> May nothing stop its course.

On the final evening, light the last stick (cone) of incense and the last anointed candle, and recite the spell. Dab a bit of oil on the last incantation paper. Recite the words on the incantation paper, light it from the candle flame, drop it into the bowl, and close the spellwork with the following:

> My spell is now complete
> May the result be all I desire.

The following morning, dispose of the candle remnants by throwing them in the trash. The quartz crystal, offering, and paper ash may be kept on the altar with the remaining herb mixture, or you may wish to carry the quartz with you for good luck. Keep the spell bottle on your altar for thirty days and then put it in a safe place to protect your prosperity. Take the money offering and use it as a donation, give it to someone in need, or buy a lottery ticket. Passing on the prosperity will bring it back to you in unexpected ways. Spells manifest in many forms, so be patient as the results may not be immediate.

Financial Stability

Use this as a protection spell for your finances. With all the changes in this world, we need to find a way to bring stability to our money and keep it safe. Get a plastic bottle, fill it with water, drop in a coin, and sprinkle in herbs. Place the spell bottle on your altar during the spellwork. At the end of the spell, take the bottle and put it in the back of the freezer to keep your money "frozen" and secure.

Financial Stability Oil:
> 1 teaspoon base oil
> 8 drops frankincense essential oil
> 8 drops myrrh essential oil
> 8 drops patchouli essential oil
> 1 juniper berry

Deities: Amun, Horus, Isis, Nephthys, Renenutet.

Candle: Choose a color related to the deity or deities you will be addressing; or use black, blue, green, orange, white, or yellow, which are appropriate for all of the spells in this book.

Incense: Pennyroyal.

Suggested Herbs: Blackthorn, chili pepper, devil's shoestring, marshmallow, tulip.

Offerings: Coins, dollar bills.

Incantation Paper Inscription: As this paper burns, protect all I have accumulated.

Spell Directions

Take a pinch of herbs and sprinkle or blow it onto your altar.

Recite the following invocation:

> Open my mind
> Open my heart
> To all the strength

That lies within

Do not let fear
Halt my quest
Do not let doubt
Cloud my mind

I have the power
To bring about change
I have the ability
To possess all I desire

Steady my hand
Strengthen my resolve
Allow what I now begin
To reach its natural conclusion

I ask the power of (deity name/the ancients)
Remove all obstacles to my goal
Make my dream reality
Make my wish come true.

Place one incense stick (or cone) in the incense holder, light it, and think about the intent of your spell. If you wish to add your own words, this would be a good point at which to do so. Anoint one of the candles with oil, place it in the candleholder, light it, and recite the following incantation:

I call to the gods for wisdom and guidance
Look favorably upon my request
As I light this candle for protection
My intentions are not entirely selfish
I ask only for a good and happy life
I have tried all other avenues
And feel the only way to achieve this
Is by asking for your assistance in attaining my
goal
May my request be granted
May all good things come to pass.

Take a drop of oil and anoint the plate, then lightly rub one of the incantation papers with your oiled fingers. Take the offering, put it on the plate, and position it in front of the candle. Take a pinch of the herbs and sprinkle on the offering. Take the quartz crystal and place it with the herbs and offering on the plate. Put the remaining herbs on the altar. Recite the following spell:

Protect my money
Keep it safe
Let me know abundance
Don't make me live
In fear of loss
Let me always have stability

> My career provides
> May it remain as such
> And keep my money safe.

Take the oiled incantation paper, recite the words on the paper, light it from the candle flame, drop it in the bowl, and finish with the following:

> Now my spell begins
> May my magic find its mark.

Allow the incense and candle to burn out on their own.

Each evening, light one stick (cone) of incense, plus one anointed candle, and recite the spell. Take a dab of oil and lightly touch an incantation paper. Recite the words on the incantation paper, light it from the candle flame, drop it in the bowl, and end with the words:

> My spell has been cast
> May nothing stop its course.

On the final evening, light the last stick (cone) of incense and the last anointed candle, and recite the spell. Dab a bit of oil on the last incantation paper. Recite the words on the incantation paper, light it from the candle flame, drop it in the bowl, and close the spellwork with the following:

My spell is now complete
May the result be all I desire.

The following morning, dispose of the candle remnants by throwing them in the trash. The quartz crystal, offering, and paper ash may be kept on the altar with the remaining herb mixture, or you may wish to carry the quartz with you for good luck. Take the money offering and use it as a donation, give it to someone in need, or buy a lottery ticket. Passing on the prosperity will bring it back to you in unexpected ways. Spells manifest in many forms, so be patient as the results may not be immediate.

Clear the Way

This spell is designed to keep people from holding you back. Jealousy sometimes clouds perception and we may have people around us who are jealous of the successes we enjoy. This spell helps to keep their negative energy from affecting us.

Clear the Way Oil:

    1 teaspoon base oil
    8 drops anise essential oil
    8 drops dragon's blood essential oil
    8 drops frankincense essential oil
    3-4 pine needles

Deities: Amun, Hathor, Imhotep, Isis, Thoth.

Candle: Choose a color related to the deity or deities you will be addressing; or use black, blue, green, orange, white, or yellow, which are appropriate for all of the spells in this book.

Incense: Citronella.

Suggested Herbs: Asafoetida, chamomile, clary sage, gum mastic, heather.

Offerings: Coins, dollar bills.

Incantation Paper Inscription: As this paper burns, my way is open and clear.

Spell Directions

Take a pinch of herbs and sprinkle or blow it onto your altar.

Recite the following invocation:

> Open my mind
> Open my heart
> To all the strength
> That lies within
>
> Do not let fear
> Halt my quest
> Do not let doubt
> Cloud my mind

I have the power
To bring about change
I have the ability
To possess all I desire

Steady my hand
Strengthen my resolve
Allow what I now begin
To reach its natural conclusion

I ask the power of (deity name/the ancients)
Remove all obstacles to my goal
Make my dream reality
Make my wish come true.

Place one incense stick (or cone) in the incense holder, light it, and think about the intent of your spell. If you wish to add your own words, this would be a good point at which to do so. Anoint one of the candles with oil, place it in the candleholder, light it, and recite the following incantation:

I call to the gods for wisdom and guidance
Look favorably upon my request
As I light this candle for purification
My intentions are not entirely selfish
I ask only for a good and happy life
I have tried all other avenues

And feel the only way to achieve this
Is by asking for your assistance in attaining my
    goal
May my request be granted
May all good things come to pass.

Take a drop of oil and anoint the plate, then lightly rub one of the incantation papers with your oiled fingers. Take the offering, put it on the plate, and position it in front of the candle. Take a pinch of the herbs and sprinkle on the offering. Take the quartz crystal and place it with the herbs and offering on the plate. Put the remaining herbs on the altar until your work is complete. Recite the following spell:

Clear my way
For some may wish
To keep me from success
I won't allow
Anyone, anything
To hold me back at all
Clear my way
My time is now
To reach my highest goals.

Take the oiled incantation paper, recite the words on the paper, light it from the candle flame, drop it into the bowl, and finish with the following:

> Now my spell begins
> May my magic find its mark.

Allow the incense and candle to burn out on their own.

Each evening, light one stick (cone) of incense, plus one anointed candle, and recite the spell. Take a dab of oil and lightly touch an incantation paper. Recite the words on the incantation paper, light it from the candle flame, drop it into the bowl, and end with the words:

> My spell has been cast
> May nothing stop its course.

On the final evening, light the last stick (cone) of incense and the last anointed candle, and recite the spell. Dab a bit of oil on the last incantation paper. Recite the words on the incantation paper, light it from the candle flame, drop it into the bowl, and close the spellwork with the following:

> My spell is now complete
> May the result be all I desire.

The following morning, dispose of the candle remnants by throwing them in the trash. The quartz crystal, offering, and paper ash may be kept on the altar with the remaining herb mixture, or you may wish to carry the quartz with you for good luck. Take the money offering and use it as a donation, give it to someone in need, or buy a lottery ticket. Passing on the prosperity will bring it back to you in unexpected ways. Spells manifest in many forms, so be patient as the results may not be immediate.

Key to Success

This spell is intended to mend a business relationship that has soured. Regardless of the reasons, the only way to achieve success is to work together. This is especially helpful for partnerships, or if you work closely with another person who seems to thwart you at every turn. Take a spell bottle, fill it with liquid (such as water, vodka, or wine), drop in a coin, and sprinkle in herbs. Keep the bottle on the altar until the conclusion of the spellwork. Then remove the coin and offer it to the person. Sprinkle the liquid around your business or work area to increase success.

Key to Success Oil:

    1 teaspoon base oil
    6 drops allspice essential oil
    8 drops lavender essential oil

8 drops myrrh essential oil
1 whole clove

Deities: Bes, Horus, Seshat, Sobek, Thoth.

Candle: Choose a color related to the deity or deities you will be addressing; or use black, blue, green, orange, white, or yellow, which are appropriate for all of the spells in this book.

Incense: Sandalwood.

Suggested Herbs: Chrysanthemum, hazel, hyssop, marjoram, sycamore.

Offerings: Coins, dollar bills.

Incantation Paper Inscription: As this paper burns, may understanding and peace prevail.

Spell Directions

Take a pinch of herbs and sprinkle or blow it onto your altar.

Recite the following invocation:

> Open my mind
> Open my heart
> To all the strength
> That lies within
>
> Do not let fear
> Halt my quest
> Do not let doubt

Cloud my mind

I have the power
To bring about change
I have the ability
To possess all I desire

Steady my hand
Strengthen my resolve
Allow what I now begin
To reach its natural conclusion

I ask the power of (deity name/the ancients)
Remove all obstacles to my goal
Make my dream reality
Make my wish come true.

Place one incense stick (or cone) in the incense holder, light it, and think about the intent of your spell. If you wish to add your own words, this would be a good point at which to do so. Anoint one of the candles with oil, place it in the candleholder, light it, and recite the following incantation:

I call to the gods for wisdom and guidance
Look favorably upon my request
As I light this candle for mending fences
My intentions are not entirely selfish

> I ask only for a good and happy life
> I have tried all other avenues
> And feel the only way to achieve this
> Is by asking for your assistance in attaining my
>   goal
> May my request be granted
> May all good things come to pass.

Take a drop of oil and anoint the plate, then lightly rub one of the incantation papers with your oiled fingers. Take the offering, put it on the plate, and position it in front of the candle. Take a pinch of the herbs and sprinkle on the offering. Take the quartz crystal and place it with the herbs and offering on the plate. Put the remaining herbs on the altar. Recite the following spell:

> Clear the air
> Between (name) and myself
> Or this will just delay
> The communication
> That must occur
> To further forge ahead
> Heal the rift
> Open the path
> Which is key to my success.

Take the oiled incantation paper, recite the words on the paper, light it from the candle flame, drop it into the bowl, and finish with the following:

> Now my spell begins
> May my magic find its mark.

Allow the incense and candle to burn out on their own.

Each evening, light one stick (cone) of incense, plus one anointed candle, and recite the spell. Take a dab of oil and lightly touch an incantation paper. Recite the words on the incantation paper, light it from the candle flame, drop it into the bowl, and end with the words:

> My spell has been cast
> May nothing stop its course.

On the final evening, light the last stick (cone) of incense and the last anointed candle, and recite the spell. Dab a bit of oil on the last incantation paper. Recite the words on the incantation paper, light it from the candle flame, drop it into the bowl, and close the spellwork with the following:

> My spell is now complete
> May the result be all I desire.

The following morning, dispose of the candle remnants by throwing them in the trash. The quartz crystal, offering, and paper ash may be kept on the altar with the remaining herb mixture, or you may wish to carry the quartz with you for good luck. Take the money offering and use it as a donation, give it to someone in need, or buy a lottery ticket. Passing on the prosperity will bring it back to you in unexpected ways. Spells manifest in many forms, so be patient as the results may not be immediate.

Time to Move On

This spell aids in knowing when it is time to leave a job and venture into the great unknown. It will help to close the door on a positive note, rather than with ill will and a possible bad recommendation. You never know when you may need a reference and one should never burn bridges in business unless absolutely necessary. Take a coin, drop it into a spell bottle filled with liquid (such as water, vodka, or wine), and sprinkle in herbs. Place it on your altar during the spell. At the conclusion, take out the coin and leave it at your old job. Sprinkle some of the liquid around your work area or the building.

Time to Move On Oil:

  1 teaspoon base oil
  8 drops benzoin essential oil
  6 drops honeysuckle essential oil

8 drops myrrh essential oil
pinch of fennel seed

Deities: Horus, Isis, Nephthys, Osiris, Ptah.

Candle: Choose a color related to the deity or deities you will be addressing; or use black, blue, green, orange, white, or yellow, which are appropriate for all of the spells in this book.

Incense: Cypress.

Suggested Herbs: Bluebell, carnation, dandelion, garlic, lemon balm.

Offerings: Coins, dollar bills.

Incantation Paper Inscription: As this paper burns, help move me in a better direction.

Spell Directions

Take a pinch of herbs and sprinkle or blow it onto your altar.

Recite the following invocation:

> Open my mind
> Open my heart
> To all the strength
> That lies within
>
> Do not let fear
> Halt my quest

Do not let doubt
Cloud my mind

I have the power
To bring about change
I have the ability
To possess all I desire

Steady my hand
Strengthen my resolve
Allow what I now begin
To reach its natural conclusion

I ask the power of (deity name/the ancients)
Remove all obstacles to my goal
Make my dream reality
Make my wish come true.

Place one incense stick (or cone) in the incense holder, light it, and think about the intent of your spell. If you wish to add your own words, this would be a good point at which to do so. Anoint one of the candles with oil, place it in the candleholder, light it, and recite the following incantation:

I call to the gods for wisdom and guidance
Look favorably upon my request
As I light this candle for release

My intentions are not entirely selfish
I ask only for a good and happy life
I have tried all other avenues
And feel the only way to achieve this
Is by asking for your assistance in attaining my
    goal
May my request be granted
May all good things come to pass.

Take a drop of oil and anoint the plate, then lightly rub one of the incantation papers with your oiled fingers. Take the offering, put it on the plate, and position it in front of the candle. Take a pinch of the herbs and sprinkle on the offering. Take the quartz crystal and place it with the herbs and offering on the plate. Put the remaining herbs on the altar. Recite the following spell:

I need to know
The time is right
To let go of the past
I want my future
To shine and sparkle
Not keep me in a rut
Let me know
The time is right
To start on a new career.

Take the oiled incantation paper, recite the words on the paper, light it from the candle flame, drop it into the bowl, and finish with the following:

> Now my spell begins
> May my magic find its mark.

Allow the incense and candle to burn out on their own.

Each evening, light one stick (cone) of incense, plus one anointed candle, and recite the spell. Take a dab of oil and lightly touch an incantation paper. Recite the words on the incantation paper, light it from the candle flame, drop it into the bowl, and end with the words:

> My spell has been cast
> May nothing stop its course.

On the final evening, light the last stick (cone) of incense and the last anointed candle, and recite the spell. Dab a bit of oil on the last incantation paper. Recite the words on the incantation paper, light it from the candle flame, drop it into the bowl, and close the spellwork with the following:

> My spell is now complete
> May the result be all I desire.

The following morning, dispose of the candle remnants by throwing them in the trash. The quartz crystal, offering, and paper ash may be kept on the altar with the remaining herb mixture, or you may wish to carry the quartz with you for good luck. Take the money offering and use it as a donation, give it to someone in need, or buy a lottery ticket. Passing on the prosperity will bring it back to you in unexpected ways. Spells manifest in many forms, so be patient as the results may not be immediate.

Reversal of Fortune

Bad luck seems to be everywhere and it always costs you something. Money is tight and it is so easy to pull out the plastic. Before you get into serious financial trouble, this spell can help reverse money woes. Get a plastic container, fill it with water, and sprinkle in herbs. Take all your credit cards, except one reserved for use only in a true emergency, put them in the container, and leave it on your altar during your spellwork. When you have completed the spell, take the container and put it as far back in the freezer as possible. Do not thaw unless it is absolutely necessary.

Reversal of Fortune Oil:

    1 teaspoon base oil

    4 drops benzoin essential oil

    6 drops geranium essential oil

    6 drops orris essential oil

pinch of fenugreek seed

Deities: Horus, Isis, Khepri, Khnum, Min

Candle: Choose a color related to the deity or deities you will be addressing; or use black, blue, green, orange, white, or yellow, which are appropriate for all of the spells in this book.

Incense: Bayberry.

Suggested Herbs: Blackberry, blessed thistle, comfrey, mugwort, orris.

Offerings: Coins, dollar bills.

Incantation Paper Inscription: As this paper burns, send luck back from where it came.

Spell Directions

Take a pinch of herbs and sprinkle or blow it onto your altar.

Recite the following invocation:

> Open my mind
> Open my heart
> To all the strength
> That lies within
>
> Do not let fear
> Halt my quest
> Do not let doubt
> Cloud my mind

> I have the power
> To bring about change
> I have the ability
> To possess all I desire
>
> Steady my hand
> Strengthen my resolve
> Allow what I now begin
> To reach its natural conclusion
>
> I ask the power of (deity name/the ancients)
> Remove all obstacles to my goal
> Make my dream reality
> Make my wish come true.

Place one incense stick (or cone) in the incense holder, light it, and think about the intent of your spell. If you wish to add your own words, this would be a good point at which to do so. Anoint one of the candles with oil, place it in the candleholder, light it, and recite the following incantation:

> I call to the gods for wisdom and guidance
> Look favorably upon my request
> As I light this candle for reversing
> My intentions are not entirely selfish
> I ask only for a good and happy life
> I have tried all other avenues

And feel the only way to achieve this
Is by asking for your assistance in attaining my
    goal
May my request be granted
May all good things come to pass.

Take a drop of oil and anoint the plate, then lightly rub one of the incantation papers with your oiled fingers. Take the offering, put it on the plate, and position it in front of the candle. Take a pinch of the herbs and sprinkle on the offering. Take the quartz crystal and place it with the herbs and offering on the plate. Put the remaining herbs on the altar. Recite the following spell:

Send this evil back
From where it came
Turn all negatives
Into positive outcomes
Make my luck
Change its ill course
Uncross my crossed path
Turn my life around
I deserve all the best.

Take the oiled incantation paper, recite the words on the paper, light it from the candle flame, drop it into the bowl, and finish with the following:

Now my spell begins
May my magic find its mark.

Allow the incense and candle to burn out on their own.

Each evening, light one stick (cone) of incense, plus one anointed candle, and recite the spell. Take a dab of oil and lightly touch an incantation paper. Recite the words on the incantation paper, light it from the candle flame, drop it into the bowl, and end with the words:

My spell has been cast
May nothing stop its course.

On the final evening, light the last stick (cone) of incense and the last anointed candle, and recite the spell. Dab a bit of oil on the last incantation paper. Recite the words on the incantation paper, light it from the candle flame, drop it into the bowl, and close the spellwork with the following:

My spell is now complete
May the result be all I desire.

The following morning, dispose of the candle remnants by throwing them in the trash. The quartz crystal, offering, and paper ash may be kept on the altar with the remaining herb mixture, or you may wish to carry the quartz with you for good luck. Take the money offering and use it as a donation, give it to someone in need, or buy a lottery ticket. Passing on the prosperity will bring it back to you in unexpected ways. Spells manifest in many forms, so be patient as the results may not be immediate.

All I Can Be

Use this spell to attract success and good fortune. This spell can also be employed when approaching investors on behalf of your business, starting a creative endeavor, or even in games of chance.

All I Can Be Oil:

    1 teaspoon base oil

    4 drops allspice essential oil

    6 drops five-finger grass essential oil

    6 drops musk essential oil

    6 drops myrrh essential oil

Deities: Bes, Geb, Hapy, Isis, Renenutet.

Candle: Choose a color related to the deity or deities you will be addressing; or use black, blue, green, orange, white, or yellow, which are appropriate for all of the spells in this book.

Incense: Frankincense.

Suggested Herbs: Alfalfa, clover, lucky hand root, poppy, vanilla.

Offerings: Coins, dollar bills.

Incantation Paper Inscription: As this paper burns, my road to success is at hand.

Spell Directions

Take a pinch of herbs and sprinkle or blow it onto your altar.

Recite the following invocation:

> Open my mind
> Open my heart
> To all the strength
> That lies within
>
> Do not let fear
> Halt my quest
> Do not let doubt
> Cloud my mind
>
> I have the power
> To bring about change
> I have the ability
> To possess all I desire
>
> Steady my hand
> Strengthen my resolve
> Allow what I now begin
> To reach its natural conclusion

> I ask the power of (deity name/the ancients)
> Remove all obstacles to my goal
> Make my dream reality
> Make my wish come true.

Place one incense stick (or cone) in the incense holder, light it, and think about the intent of your spell. If you wish to add your own words, this would be a good point at which to do so. Anoint one of the candles with oil, place it in the candleholder, light it, and recite the following incantation:

> I call to the gods for wisdom and guidance
> Look favorably upon my request
> As I light this candle for success
> My intentions are not entirely selfish
> I ask only for a good and happy life
> I have tried all other avenues
> And feel the only way to achieve this
> Is by asking for your assistance in attaining my
>   goal
> May my request be granted
> May all good things come to pass.

Take a drop of oil and anoint the plate, then lightly rub one of the incantation papers with your oiled fingers. Take the offering, put it on the plate, and position it in

front of the candle. Take a pinch of the herbs and sprinkle on the offering. Take the quartz crystal and place it with the herbs and offering on the plate. Put the remaining herbs on the altar until your work is complete. Recite the following spell:

> Good fortune is within my reach
> Help me to attain
> The highest levels of success
> In my career
> In my relationships
> And in my life
> Nothing can hold me back
> From being successful
> Because I have the power
> To make it all happen.

Take the oiled incantation paper, recite the words on the paper, light it from the candle flame, drop it in the bowl, and finish with the following:

> Now my spell begins
> May my magic find its mark.

Allow the incense and candle to burn out on their own.

Each evening, light one stick (cone) of incense, plus one anointed candle, and recite the spell. Take a dab of oil and lightly touch an incantation paper. Recite the

words on the incantation paper, light it from the candle flame, drop it in the bowl, and end with the words:

> My spell has been cast
> May nothing stop its course.

On the final evening, light the last stick (cone) of incense and the last anointed candle, and recite the spell. Dab a bit of oil on the last incantation paper. Recite the words on the incantation paper, light it from the candle flame, drop it in the bowl, and close the spellwork with the following:

> My spell is now complete
> May the result be all I desire.

The following morning, dispose of the candle remnants by throwing them in the trash. The quartz crystal, offering, and paper ash may be kept on the altar with the remaining herb mixture, or you may wish to carry the quartz with you for good luck. Take the money offering and use it as a donation, give it to someone in need, or buy a lottery ticket. Passing on the prosperity will bring it back to you in unexpected ways. Spells manifest in many forms, so be patient as the results may not be immediate.

Coast Along

Use this spell when life changes around you and you have little control over the changes. New bosses arrive with their own ideas and, with downsizing, many people find themselves overwhelmed doing the jobs of their former coworkers as well as their own. This spell can help you keep things in perspective or help you to see what path to take. Get a bottle, fill it with liquid (such as water, vodka, or wine), drop in a coin, and sprinkle with herbs. Keep it on your altar during the spellwork and, when the spell is concluded, sprinkle some of the liquid around your workplace.

Coast Along Oil:

> 1 teaspoon base oil
> 6 drops allspice essential oil
> 8 drops myrrh essential oil
> 8 drops rose essential oil
> pinch of sesame seed

Deities: Hathor, Heqet, Horus, Osiris, Ptah.

Candle: Choose a color related to the deity or deities you will be addressing; or use black, blue, green, orange, white, or yellow, which are appropriate for all of the spells in this book.

Incense: Myrrh.

Suggested Herbs: Chives, cyclamen, elecampane, hyacinth, passionflower.

Offerings: Coins, dollar bills.

Incantation Paper Inscription: As this paper burns, may the path ahead be free from stress and worry.

Spell Directions

Take a pinch of herbs and sprinkle or blow it onto your altar.

Recite the following invocation:

> Open my mind
> Open my heart
> To all the strength
> That lies within
>
> Do not let fear
> Halt my quest
> Do not let doubt
> Cloud my mind
>
> I have the power
> To bring about change
> I have the ability
> To possess all I desire

Steady my hand
Strengthen my resolve
Allow what I now begin
To reach its natural conclusion

I ask the power of (deity name/the ancients)
Remove all obstacles to my goal
Make my dream reality
Make my wish come true.

Place one incense stick (or cone) in the incense holder, light it, and think about the intent of your spell. If you wish to add your own words, this would be a good point at which to do so. Anoint one of the candles with oil, place it in the candleholder, light it, and recite the following incantation:

I call to the gods for wisdom and guidance
Look favorably upon my request
As I light this candle for transitions
My intentions are not entirely selfish
I ask only for a good and happy life
I have tried all other avenues
And feel the only way to achieve this
Is by asking for your assistance in attaining my
    goal
May my request be granted

May all good things come to pass.

Take a drop of oil and anoint the plate, then lightly rub one of the incantation papers with your oiled fingers. Take the offering, put it on the plate, and position it in front of the candle. Take a pinch of the herbs and sprinkle on the offering. Take the quartz crystal and place it with the herbs and offering on the plate. Put the remaining herbs on the altar. Recite the following spell:

> I feel the changes
> In my life
> Are not mine to control
> I may adapt
> Or attempt to fight
> I may just coast along
> Help me cope
> Help me make
> The choice that's best for me.

Take the oiled incantation paper, recite the words on the paper, light it from the candle flame, drop it in the bowl, and finish with the following:

> Now my spell begins
> May my magic find its mark.

Allow the incense and candle to burn out on their own.

Each evening, light one stick (cone) of incense, plus one anointed candle, and recite the spell. Take a dab of oil and lightly touch an incantation paper. Recite the words on the incantation paper, light it from the candle flame, drop it in the bowl, and end with the words:

> My spell has been cast
> May nothing stop its course.

On the final evening, light the last stick (cone) of incense and the last anointed candle, and recite the spell. Dab a bit of oil on the last incantation paper. Recite the words on the incantation paper, light it from the candle flame, drop it in the bowl, and close the spellwork with the following:

> My spell is now complete
> May the result be all I desire.

The following morning, dispose of the candle remnants by throwing them in the trash. The quartz crystal, offering, and paper ash may be kept on the altar with the remaining herb mixture, or you may wish to carry the quartz with you for good luck. Take the money offering and use it as a donation, give it to someone in need, or buy a lottery ticket. Passing on the prosperity will bring it back to you in unexpected ways. Spells manifest in many forms, so be patient as the results may not be immediate.

Dreams of Success

Use this spell to achieve your fondest wish for success—don't dream it, be it! Trust me when I say that I never thought of myself as an author, but now I don't know how I ever got along without writing. Whatever your dreams of success, you can make it happen.

Dreams of Success Oil:

    1 teaspoon base oil

    8 drops lavender essential oil

    8 drops rose essential oil

    8 drops vanilla essential oil

    1 pumpkin seed

Deities: Amun, Khepri, Min, Mut, Ptah.

Candle: Choose a color related to the deity or deities you will be addressing; or use black, blue, green, orange, white, or yellow, which are appropriate for all of the spells in this book.

Incense: Musk.

Suggested Herbs: Chocolate, daisy, pomegranate, pumpkin, rice.

Offerings: Coins, dollar bills, business cards, or whatever represents your success.

Incantation Paper Inscription: As this paper burns, make my dreams come true and my wishes real.

Spell Directions

Take a pinch of herbs and sprinkle or blow it onto your altar.

Recite the following invocation:

> Open my mind
> Open my heart
> To all the strength
> That lies within
>
> Do not let fear
> Halt my quest
> Do not let doubt
> Cloud my mind
>
> I have the power
> To bring about change
> I have the ability
> To possess all I desire
>
> Steady my hand
> Strengthen my resolve
> Allow what I now begin
> To reach its natural conclusion

> I ask the power of (deity name/the ancients)
> Remove all obstacles to my goal
> Make my dream reality
> Make my wish come true.

Place one incense stick (or cone) in the incense holder, light it, and think about the intent of your spell. If you wish to add your own words, this would be a good point at which to do so. Anoint one of the candles with oil, place it in the candleholder, light it, and recite the following incantation:

> I call to the gods for wisdom and guidance
> Look favorably upon my request
> As I light this candle for my special wish
> My intentions are not entirely selfish
> I ask only for a good and happy life
> I have tried all other avenues
> And feel the only way to achieve this
> Is by asking for your assistance in attaining my
>   goal
> May my request be granted
> May all good things come to pass.

Take a drop of oil and anoint the plate, then lightly rub one of the incantation papers with your oiled fingers. Take the offering, put it on or next to the plate, and position it in front of the candle. Take a pinch of the herbs and sprinkle on the offering. Take the quartz crystal and place it with the herbs and offering on the plate. Put the remaining herbs on the altar. Recite the following spell:

> I dream each day
> For (state purpose)
> And fear it will never be
> I need to take
> A chance or two
> To make my wish come true
> I'll take the first step
> No matter the risk
> To make my dream of success a reality.

Take the oiled incantation paper, recite the words on the paper, light it from the candle flame, drop it in the bowl, and finish with the following:

> Now my spell begins
> May my magic find its mark.

Allow the incense and candle to burn out on their own.

Each evening, light one stick (cone) of incense, plus one anointed candle, and recite the spell. Take a dab of oil and lightly touch an incantation paper. Recite the words on the incantation paper, light it from the candle flame, drop it in the bowl, and end with the words:

> My spell has been cast
> May nothing stop its course.

On the final evening, light the last stick (cone) of incense and the last anointed candle, and recite the spell. Dab a bit of oil on the last incantation paper. Recite the words on the incantation paper, light it from the candle flame, drop it in the bowl, and close the spellwork with the following:

> My spell is now complete
> May the result be all I desire.

The following morning, dispose of the candle remnants by throwing them in the trash. The quartz crystal, offering, and paper ash may be kept on the altar with the remaining herb mixture, or you may wish to carry the quartz with you for good luck. If the offering was an expression of what success means to you, keep it prominently displayed to remind you each and every day of what you are striving for. If the offering was money, use it as a donation, give it to someone in need, or buy a lottery ticket. Passing on the prosperity will bring it back to you in unexpected ways. Spells manifest in many forms, so be patient as the results may not be immediate.

Success at Last

We sometimes forget to thank the gods when things turn out the way we want, but we are often the first to complain when they do not. This spell requires very little, but it should be used as a thank-you for a successful job search/interview/presentation/contract.

Success at Last Oil:

    1 teaspoon base oil
    6 drops cinnamon essential oil
    8 drops lilac essential oil
    8 drops rose essential oil
    1 allspice berry

    Deities: Bes, Horus, Isis, Ptah, Thoth.
    Candle: One white or green candle.
    Incense: Sandalwood.
    Offerings: Coins, dollar bills, bread, beer or wine.
    Incantation Paper Inscription: As this paper burns, my goal has been reached.

Spell Directions

Place the incense stick (or cone) in the incense holder and light it. Anoint the candle with oil, place it in the candleholder, and light it. Take a drop of oil and anoint the plate, then lightly rub the incantation paper with your oiled fingers. Take the offering, put it on the plate, and position it in front of the candle. Recite the following spell:

> The waiting is over
> No more needs to be said
> I have finally reached the goal
> I've worked so hard to attain
> Now I can breathe
> A sigh of relief
> I knew I could do it
> I knew all along
> Success would at last be mine.

If you wish to add your own words, this would be a good point at which to do so. Take the oiled incantation paper, recite the words on the paper, light it from the candle flame, drop it into the bowl, and finish with the following:

> My success is complete
> Thank you for my magic.

Allow the incense and candle to burn out on their own.

The following morning, dispose of the candle remnants by throwing them in the trash. If the offering was food or liquid, pour it outside as a libation to the gods. If the offering was money, use it to make a difference in the world.

FIVE

Emergency Financial Spells

It's a fact of life that the economy is in trouble. The federal debt is in the trillions of dollars; state debt has resulted in office closures, service cutbacks, and issuing IOUs to vendors; cities base their budgets on tax revenue projections and, when those fall short, they are forced to cut back on programs and services. As a nation of consumers, maybe now is the time to change our mindsets. Instead of pulling out the plastic, pay cash. Instead of buying what you *want*, buy only what you *need*. It can be very rewarding to work toward acquiring something, rather than just buying it on a whim.

For those of you in deep financial difficulty, it may seem there is no way out. But trust me—there is light at the end of the tunnel. We all go through periods of financial instability, and it can really play havoc with your self-esteem and your relationships. The following spells are meant to help alleviate the stress, depression, and hopelessness that accompany a personal financial meltdown. Think of it as a magical bailout for you.

Each spell comes with a little practical advice to help guide you in a better direction, regardless of what your situation may be. I promise not to preach, and my bailout comes with no strings attached and nothing to be repaid. I purposely designed these spells to be relatively painless, and all are to be performed in just one evening. When you are in financial difficulty, you have enough stress in your life; a quick and easy spell will help you begin to take back your life.

Debt Control

This spell is designed to get a handle on debts before they overwhelm you, or before loss of income occurs. Practical advice: put the credit cards away! It may help to keep a log of everything you buy for one week to see where your money is really going. It may surprise you.

Debt Control Oil:
    1 teaspoon base oil
    2 drops cinnamon essential oil

4 drops five-finger grass essential oil
6 drops honeysuckle essential oil
6 drops jasmine essential oil
6 drops patchouli essential oil

Deities: Ma'at, Nephthys, Osiris, Ptah, Seshat, Thoth.
Candle: One: choose from green, yellow, white, or blue.
Incense: Pine.
Offerings: Coins, dollar bills, credit cards, overdue bills, allspice berries, wine or beer.

Spell Directions
Place the incense stick (or cone) in the incense holder and light it. Recite the following:

> I need help
> I need it now

Anoint the candle with oil, place it in the candleholder, and light it. If you wish to add your own words, this would be the time. Take a drop of oil and anoint the plate. Take the offering, put it on the plate or next to it, and position it in front of the candle. Recite the following spell:

> Debts, out of control
> Spent before it's earned
> And still never enough

Now is the time
No more excuses
To delay could spell disaster
Stop and think
Make the right choice
And regain control.

Allow the incense and candle to burn out on their own.

The following morning, dispose of the candle remnants by throwing them in the trash. If the offering was food or liquid, pour it outside as a libation to the gods. If the offering was money, use it to make a difference in your situation; if it was an overdue bill or legal document, take care of it promptly to avoid further problems. If the offering was a credit card, leave it on the altar—if it's not with you, you can't use it.

Workable Budget

This spell is designed to help you cut unnecessary expenses. Practical advice: cut back to one latte a week, bring a lunch to work, and look at where you can save on cable, Internet, and cell phone services. Don't drive to work every day; try carpooling, biking, or public transportation if available. If you have a practical skill, try bartering for services. You may be amazed at how much you can save if you look at your expenses with your head instead of with your heart.

Workable Budget Oil:

>   1 teaspoon base oil
>   2 drops allspice essential oil
>   4 drops five-finger grass essential oil
>   6 drops honeysuckle essential oil
>   6 drops jasmine essential oil
>   6 drops patchouli essential oil

Deities: Ma'at, Nephthys, Osiris, Ptah, Seshat, Thoth.

Candle: One; choose from green, yellow, white, or blue.

Incense: Lavender.

Offerings: Aniseed, tobacco, coins, dollar bills, credit cards, overdue bills, wine or beer.

Spell Directions

Place the incense stick (or cone) in the incense holder and light it. Recite the following:

>   I need help
>   I need it now

Anoint the candle with oil, place it in the candleholder, and light it. If you wish to add your own words, this would be the time. Take a drop of oil and anoint the plate. Take the offering, put it on the plate or next to it, and position it in front of the candle. Recite the following spell:

> Cut hard and deep
> It really needs to hurt
> In order to make a difference
> Do not despair
> Do not be tempted
> To slip back into old habits
> It is not forever
> It needs to be done
> Before it is too late to change.

Allow the incense and candle to burn out on their own.

The following morning, dispose of the candle remnants by throwing them in the trash. If the offering was food or liquid, pour it outside as a libation to the gods. If the offering was money, use it to make a difference in your situation; if it was an overdue bill or legal document, take care of it promptly to avoid further problems. If the offering was a credit card, leave it on the altar—if it's not with you, you can't use it.

Surviving Layoffs

In these hard economic times, many of us are faced with the reality of cutbacks, layoffs, downsizing, and outsourcing. Practical advice: if you are carrying credit card debt, call your creditors as soon as you learn you will be laid off and see if you can work out a payment arrangement with them. Some companies will negotiate with you, and some don't give a rat's behind about you and your financial situation. And with millions of people out of work nationwide, don't be ashamed to apply for unemployment, even if you think you may only be out of work for several weeks; some income is always better than no income.

Surviving Layoffs Oil:

    1 teaspoon base oil
    4 drops five-finger grass essential oil
    2 drops frankincense essential oil
    6 drops honeysuckle essential oil
    6 drops jasmine essential oil
    6 drops patchouli essential oil

Deities: Ma'at, Nephthys, Osiris, Ptah, Seshat, Thoth.

Candle: One; choose from green, yellow, white, or blue.

Incense: Rose.

Offerings: Coins, dollar bills, basil, star anise, credit cards, overdue bills, wine or beer.

Spell Directions

Place the incense stick (or cone) in the incense holder and light it. Recite the following:

> I need help
> I need it now

Anoint the candle with oil, place it in the candleholder, and light it. If you wish to add your own words, this would be the time. Take a drop of oil and anoint the plate. Take the offering, put it on the plate or next to it, and position it in front of the candle. Recite the following spell:

> No time to wallow
> In self-pity or doubt
> I need to find a solution
> I am not alone
> Others share my fate
> Yet I won't let this overwhelm me
> Give me the strength
> Shore up my willpower
> To deal with this temporary setback.

Allow the incense and candle to burn out on their own.

The following morning, dispose of the candle remnants by throwing them in the trash. If the offering was food or liquid, pour it outside as a libation to the gods. If the offering was money, use it to make a difference in your situation; if it was an overdue bill or legal document, take care of it promptly to avoid further problems. If the offering was a credit card, leave it on the altar—if it's not with you, you can't use it.

Alternate Income

Some people are fortunate to rebound quickly in tough economic times, while others don't have a financial cushion to help them through. If you have the means to "wait it out" until you find a new job, all the more power to you. If not, why not create your own job? There are literally hundreds of ways to make money online or with a home-based business. Do your homework, research the market in your area, and don't fall for any deal where you have to put out money up front. Approach local businesses and offer your unique talents on a freelance basis (which does not mean free), attend Chamber of Commerce events and network to get your name out, and don't forget to tell everyone you meet that you are looking for work. You never know when and where your next job may come from.

Alternate Income Oil:

    1 teaspoon base oil
    4 drops five-finger grass essential oil
    6 drops honeysuckle essential oil

6 drops jasmine essential oil

2 drops orange essential oil

6 drops patchouli essential oil

Deities: Ma'at, Nephthys, Osiris, Ptah, Seshat, Thoth.

Candle: One; choose from green, yellow, white, or blue.

Incense: Ylang-ylang.

Offerings: Coriander, oregano, coins, dollar bills, credit cards, overdue bills, wine or beer.

Spell Directions

Place the incense stick (or cone) in the incense holder and light it. Recite the following:

> I need help
> I need it now

Anoint the candle with oil, place it in the candleholder, and light it. If you wish to add your own words, this would be the time. Take a drop of oil and anoint the plate. Take the offering, put it on the plate or next to it, and position it in front of the candle. Recite the following spell:

> I have so much to offer
> I am skilled beyond my years
> Competition is fierce

Times are bleak
And my patience is at an end
I will seize the opportunity
To strike out on my own
The time is right
The time is now
To create the job of my dreams.

Allow the incense and candle to burn out on their own.

The following morning, dispose of the candle remnants by throwing them in the trash. If the offering was food or liquid, pour it outside as a libation to the gods. If the offering was money, use it to make a difference in your situation; if it was an overdue bill or legal document, take care of it promptly to avoid further problems. If the offering was a credit card, leave it on the altar—if it's not with you, you can't use it.

Choosing an Attorney

I hope that you will not need this spell, or the next two, but they are important to include. Some financial problems eventually result in legal action, and you may need an attorney to protect your interests. Practical advice: many attorneys will offer a first visit free, and provide you with necessary information. When choosing an attorney, make sure you feel comfortable with him or her; if you don't, keep looking until you find the one that's right for you. Don't sign anything you do not fully understand, and never feel pressured to accept a settlement.

Choosing an Attorney Oil:

    1 teaspoon base oil
    4 drops five-finger grass essential oil
    6 drops honeysuckle essential oil
    6 drops jasmine essential oil
    2 drops myrrh essential oil
    6 drops patchouli essential oil

Deities: Ma'at, Nephthys, Osiris, Ptah, Seshat, Thoth.

Candle: One; choose from green, yellow, white, or blue.

Incense: Bergamot.

Offerings: Lemon, violet, coins, dollar bills, credit cards, overdue bills, wine or beer.

Spell Directions

Place the incense stick (or cone) in the incense holder and light it. Recite the following:

    I need help
    I need it now

Anoint the candle with oil, place it in the candleholder, and light it. If you wish to add your own words, this would be the time. Take a drop of oil and anoint the plate. Take the offering, put it on the plate or next to it, and position it in front of the candle. Recite the following spell:

> The choice I make
> May be quick
> Or may take time and effort
> I need to know
> I need to feel
> The choice is right for me
> Help me choose
> Well and wisely
> Or the results may be devastating.

Allow the incense and candle to burn out on their own.

The following morning, dispose of the candle remnants by throwing them in the trash. If the offering was food or liquid, pour it outside as a libation to the gods. If the offering was money, use it to make a difference in your situation; if it was an overdue bill or legal document, take care of it promptly to avoid further problems. If the offering was a credit card, leave it on the altar—if it's not with you, you can't use it.

Bankruptcy

If your situation is really dire, the only option you may have available is to file bankruptcy. I am not a legal expert, so you will need to do your own research, at your local library or on the Internet, regarding the laws of your particular state. Practical advice: if your financial situation is affecting others, you need to sit down with them, be honest, and decide what would be the best course of action for everyone concerned. Only you can decide if filing bankruptcy is right for you in your particular situation. But if you decide to do so, this spell is intended to ease the process as much as possible.

Bankruptcy Oil:

    1 teaspoon base oil

    4 drops five-finger grass essential oil

    6 drops honeysuckle essential oil

    6 drops jasmine essential oil

    6 drops patchouli essential oil

    1 drop vetivert essential oil

Deities: Ma'at, Nephthys, Osiris, Ptah, Seshat, Thoth.

Candle: One; choose from green, yellow, white, or blue.

Incense: Vetivert.

Offerings: Nutmeg, spearmint, coins, dollar bills, legal documents, wine or beer.

Spell Directions

Place the incense stick (or cone) in the incense holder and light it. Recite the following:

> I need help
> I need it now

Anoint the candle with oil, place it in the candleholder, and light it. If you wish to add your own words, this would be the time. Take a drop of oil and anoint the plate. Take the offering, put it on the plate or next to it, and position it in front of the candle. Recite the following spell:

> I am not a bad person
> I am not a failure
> Though that is how I feel
> I took too long
> To take control
> Now I have only one way out
> I will come through
> I am smart and strong
> And I won't make the same mistakes again.

Allow the incense and candle to burn out on their own.

The following morning, dispose of the candle remnants by throwing them in the trash. If the offering was food or liquid, pour it outside as a libation to the gods. If the offering was money, use it to make a difference in your situation. If the offering was a legal document, take care of it promptly to avoid further problems.

Foreclosure

One of the most devastating events in one's life is the loss of one's home. This spell is designed to help you forestall foreclosure if you are able to work with the bank, or to help you accept the loss of your home if negotiation is not possible. Practical advice: don't stick your head in the sand and try to ignore the issue. Find out about your options *early* in the foreclosure process.

Foreclosure Oil:

> 1 teaspoon base oil
> 4 drops five-finger grass essential oil
> 6 drops honeysuckle essential oil
> 6 drops jasmine essential oil
> 6 drops patchouli essential oil
> 2 drops sandalwood essential oil

Deities: Ma'at, Nephthys, Osiris, Ptah, Seshat, Thoth.
Candle: One; choose from green, yellow, white, or blue.

Incense: Sage.

Offerings: Dill, peppermint, coins, dollar bills, legal documents, wine or beer.

Spell Directions

Place the incense stick (or cone) in the incense holder and light it. Recite the following:

> I need help
> I need it now

Anoint the candle with oil, place it in the candleholder, and light it. If you wish to add your own words, this would be the time. Take a drop of oil and anoint the plate. Take the offering, put it on the plate or next to it, and position it in front of the candle. Recite the following spell:

> I've done everything in my power
> To hold off the coming storm
> But I made some bad choices
> Which I can no longer avoid
> A house is but a structure
> For comfort and for peace
> I don't know how
> But I'll make it through
> To find my home again.

Allow the incense and candle to burn out on their own.

The following morning, dispose of the candle remnants by throwing them in the trash. If the offering was food or liquid, pour it outside as a libation to the gods. If the offering was money, use it to make a difference in your situation. If the offering was a legal document, take care of it promptly to avoid further problems.

APPENDIX A

Ingredient Correspondences for
Prosperity Spells

Note that items marked with an asterisk (*) are poisonous; do not ingest!

Acacia (Gum Arabic): Attraction, beginnings, blessing, communication, creativity, dispelling negativity, endings, inspiration, job hunting, magic power, overcoming obstacles, peace, power, prosperity, protection, purification, reconciliation, release, success, transitions, wishes. Deities: Bast, Osiris, Ra.

Acorn: Attraction, blessing, creativity, inspiration, job hunting, overcoming obstacles, power, prosperity, protection, success, transitions.

Adder's Tongue: Beginnings, dispelling negativity, endings, inspiration, magic power, overcoming obstacles, power, protection, release, reversing, transitions.

Agrimony: Attraction, banishing, blessing, dispelling negativity, endings, job hunting, overcoming obstacles, power, prosperity, protection, purification, reversing, success.

Alder: Banishing, blessing, communication, endings, inspiration, magic power, overcoming obstacles, power, protection, reversing.

Alfalfa: Attraction, blessing, creativity, dispelling negativity, inspiration, job hunting, overcoming obstacles, prosperity, protection, success, transitions.

Alkanet: Attraction, banishing, blessing, creativity, dispelling negativity, inspiration, job hunting, prosperity, protection, purification, reversing, success.

Allspice (Pimento): Attraction, beginnings, blessing, communication, creativity, dispelling negativity, inspiration, job hunting, legal matters, magic power, overcoming obstacles, power, prosperity, reconciliation, success.

Almond: Attraction, beginnings, blessing, communication, creativity, endings, inspiration, job hunting, peace, prosperity, reconciliation, reversing, success, transitions. Deity: Thoth.

Aloe: Attraction, banishing, beginnings, blessing, dispelling negativity, endings, job hunting, peace, power, prosperity, protection, purification, reconciliation, reversing, success. Egyptians used it in embalming.

Amaranth: Beginnings, blessing, communication, endings, inspiration, overcoming obstacles, peace, protection, reconciliation, release, transitions.

Ambergris: Magic power, power.

Ammonia: Banishing, endings, overcoming obstacles, protection, purification, reversing.

Anemone: Beginnings, endings, peace, power, protection, release, transitions.

Angelica: Attraction, banishing, beginnings, blessing, communication, creativity, dispelling negativity, endings, inspiration, job hunting, legal matters, magic power, overcoming obstacles, peace, power, prosperity, protection, purification, reversing, success, wishes.

Aniseed: Attraction, banishing, beginnings, blessing, communication, creativity, dispelling negativity, endings, inspiration, job hunting, legal matters, peace, prosperity, protection, purification, reconciliation, success, wishes.

Apple: Beginnings, blessing, communication, creativity, dispelling negativity, inspiration, magic power, peace, power, prosperity, protection, success, transitions, wishes. Apple cider may be used as a substitute for blood.

Apricot: Communication, creativity, peace, reconciliation.

Arrowroot: Attraction, blessing, inspiration, job hunting, prosperity, protection, reversing, success.

Asafoetida: Banishing, dispelling negativity, endings, legal matters, magic power, overcoming obstacles, protection, purification, release, reversing. Has an incredibly foul odor.

Ash: Attraction, banishing, blessing, communication, creativity, dispelling negativity, endings, inspiration, job hunting, magic power, overcoming obstacles, peace, power, prosperity, protection, purification, reversing, success, transitions, wishes.

Ashes: Banishing, communication, creativity, endings, inspiration, overcoming obstacles, prosperity, protection, purification, reconciliation, release, transitions, wishes.

Aspen: Communication, power, reversing.

Asphodel: Blessing, endings, peace, purification, release, transitions.

Aster: Banishing, dispelling negativity, endings, peace, power, reversing.

Avens: Banishing, blessing, dispelling negativity, endings, protection, purification, reversing.

Avocado: Attraction, magic power, peace, power, prosperity. This is often referred to as the Egyptian persea, though the persea may well have been another plant.

Bachelor's Buttons (Cornflower): Banishing, communication, creativity, dispelling negativity, endings, inspiration, magic power, overcoming obstacles, peace, purification, release, reversing.

Baking Soda: Banishing, dispelling negativity, endings, protection, purification.

Balm of Gilead: Attraction, communication, creativity, inspiration, job hunting, power, prosperity, protection, success, wishes.

Bamboo: Attraction, banishing, beginnings, blessing, dispelling negativity, endings, job hunting, overcoming obstacles, power, prosperity, protection, reversing, success, transitions, wishes.

Banana: Attraction, communication, creativity, endings, inspiration, job hunting, prosperity, protection, release, success, transitions.

Barley: Attraction, creativity, dispelling negativity, inspiration, job hunting, prosperity, protection, success, transitions, wishes.

Basil: Attraction, banishing, blessing, communication, creativity, dispelling negativity, endings, inspiration, job hunting, legal matters, magic power, overcoming obstacles, peace, power, prosperity, protection, purification, reconciliation, release, reversing, success, transitions, wishes.

Bay (Bay Laurel, Laurel): Attraction, banishing, blessing, communication, creativity, dispelling negativity, endings, inspiration, job hunting, legal matters, magic power, overcoming obstacles, peace, power, prosperity, protection, purification, reconciliation, release, reversing, success, transitions, wishes.

Bayberry: Attraction, blessing, job hunting, legal matters, magic power, peace, power, prosperity, protection, purification, reconciliation, reversing, success, wishes.

Beech: Attraction, communication, creativity, inspiration, job hunting, legal matters, peace, prosperity, protection, success, wishes.

Beer: Banishing, dispelling negativity, endings, protection, purification, release, reversing. Used as an offering in spellwork and rituals.

Beet: Attraction, banishing, job hunting, prosperity. Used to create a magical ink or as a substitute for blood.

Belladonna (Deadly Nightshade)*: Banishing, blessing, communication, creativity, dispelling negativity, endings, inspiration, legal matters, magic power, overcoming obstacles, protection, purification, release, reversing, transitions. One of the ingredients in flying ointment.

Benzoin (Styrax): Attraction, banishing, beginnings, blessing, creativity, dispelling negativity, endings, inspiration, job hunting, legal matters, magic power, overcoming obstacles, peace, power, prosperity, protection, purification, reconciliation, release, reversing, success, transitions, wishes. Deity: Mut.

Bergamot: Attraction, job hunting, legal matters, overcoming obstacles, peace, power, prosperity, protection, reconciliation, reversing, success, wishes.

Birch: Banishing, beginnings, blessing, communication, creativity, dispelling negativity, endings, inspiration, magic power, overcoming obstacles, peace, power, protection, purification, release.

Bistort: Attraction, banishing, blessing, communication, creativity, dispelling negativity, inspiration, job hunting, prosperity, success.

Bittersweet (Woody Nightshade)*: Banishing, dispelling negativity, endings, legal matters, magic power, overcoming obstacles, power, protection, purification, reversing, transitions, wishes.

Black Cohosh: Attraction, banishing, dispelling negativity, endings, job hunting, overcoming obstacles, peace, power, prosperity, protection, reversing, success, wishes. Do not use if pregnant.

Black Hellebore*: Banishing, blessing, creativity, dispelling negativity, endings, magic power, overcoming obstacles, power, protection, reversing.

Black Pepper: Banishing, dispelling negativity, endings, legal matters, magic power, overcoming obstacles, power, protection, purification, release, reversing, wishes.

Blackberry: Attraction, blessing, job hunting, magic power, overcoming obstacles, prosperity, protection, reversing, success. Used to create a magical ink.

Blackthorn: Banishing, dispelling negativity, endings, magic power, protection, purification, release, reversing, wishes. Used to cause havoc. Thorns may be used to carve hexing candles.

Blessed Thistle: Banishing, blessing, dispelling negativity, endings, magic power, overcoming obstacles, peace, power, prosperity, protection, purification, reversing.

Blood: Communication, legal matters, magic power, power, protection. Used in sympathetic magic to represent the person you wish to influence.

Bloodroot*: Banishing, dispelling negativity, endings, overcoming obstacles, peace, power, protection, purification, reversing.

Bluebell: Blessing, endings, legal matters, release, transitions.

Blueberry: Attraction, creativity, dispelling negativity, inspiration, job hunting, overcoming obstacles, power, prosperity, protection, success. Used to create a magical ink.

Borage: Attraction, beginnings, communication, creativity, inspiration, job hunting, overcoming obstacles, peace, power, prosperity, protection, reversing, success, transitions.

Box*: Endings, overcoming obstacles, release, transitions.

Bracken Fern: Attraction, banishing, blessing, communication, creativity, dispelling negativity, endings, inspiration, job hunting, magic power, overcoming obstacles, power, prosperity, protection, purification, reversing, success, wishes.

Broom*: Attraction, banishing, beginnings, blessing, communication, creativity, dispelling negativity, endings, inspiration, job hunting, magic power, overcoming obstacles, prosperity, protection, purification, reversing, success.

Bryony*: Attraction, prosperity, protection, success. May be used in place of mandrake.

Buckeye*: Attraction, blessing, job hunting, prosperity, reversing, success, wishes. Seeds are poisonous.

Buckthorn (Cascara Segrada)*: Attraction, banishing, blessing, communication, dispelling negativity, endings, job hunting, legal matters, prosperity, protection, purification, reversing, success, wishes.

Buckwheat: Attraction, banishing, dispelling negativity, endings, job hunting, prosperity, protection, success.

Burdock: Banishing, dispelling negativity, endings, inspiration, power, protection, purification, reversing.

Business Card: Used in sympathetic magic to represent the person or organization you wish to influence.

Calamus (Sweet Sedge, Sweet Flag)*: Attraction, blessing, communication, job hunting, magic power, peace, power, prosperity, protection, purification, reconciliation, reversing, success.

Camellia: Attraction, dispelling negativity, job hunting, overcoming obstacles, peace, prosperity, reversing, success, wishes.

Cantaloupe: Overcoming obstacles, wishes.

Caraway: Attraction, communication, creativity, dispelling negativity, inspiration, job hunting, legal matters, magic power, overcoming obstacles, power, prosperity, protection, purification, reconciliation, success, wishes.

Cardamom: Attraction, blessing, communication, creativity, inspiration, job hunting, overcoming obstacles, prosperity, success, wishes.

Carnation: Banishing, blessing, communication, creativity, dispelling negativity, endings, inspiration, legal matters, magic power, overcoming obstacles, peace,

power, protection, purification, release, reversing,
transitions, wishes.

Carob: Beginnings, blessing, dispelling negativity,
magic power, protection.

Carrot: Creativity, inspiration, overcoming obstacles,
power.

Cat Hair: Attraction, banishing (black cat hair), blessing, endings (black cat hair), job hunting, magic
power, power, prosperity, protection (gray cat hair),
success, wishes.

Cat Whiskers: Attraction, job hunting, wishes.

Catnip: Banishing, blessing, creativity, dispelling negativity, endings, inspiration, job hunting, magic power,
overcoming obstacles, peace, power, prosperity, protection, reconciliation, release, reversing, success, wishes.
Use with dragon's blood to break a bad habit. Deities:
Bast, Sekhmet.

Cayenne Pepper: Banishing, beginnings, communication, dispelling negativity, endings, overcoming obstacles, power, protection, release, reversing, transitions.
Used to cause havoc.

Cedar: Attraction, banishing, blessing, communication, dispelling negativity, endings, inspiration, job hunting, legal matters, magic power, overcoming obstacles, peace, power, prosperity, protection, purification, release, reversing, success.

Celandine: Banishing, dispelling negativity, endings, inspiration, legal matters, overcoming obstacles, peace, power, protection, release, reversing, success, transitions.

Celery: Communication, creativity, inspiration, overcoming obstacles.

Centaury: Banishing, dispelling negativity, endings, inspiration, magic power, overcoming obstacles, power, protection, purification, release, reversing.

Chamomile: Attraction, banishing, blessing, communication, creativity, dispelling negativity, endings, job hunting, legal matters, magic power, overcoming obstacles, peace, power, prosperity, protection, purification, reconciliation, reversing, success, wishes. Do not use if pregnant.

Cherry: Attraction, banishing, communication, creativity, dispelling negativity, endings, inspiration, job hunting, legal matters, overcoming obstacles, peace, prosperity, reversing, success, wishes. Use for creating a magical ink or as a substitute for blood.

Chervil: Beginnings, communication, creativity, dispelling negativity, endings, inspiration, magic power, peace, release, reversing, transitions.

Chestnut: Attraction, banishing, blessing, communication, dispelling negativity, endings, inspiration, legal matters, overcoming obstacles, prosperity, reversing, wishes.

Chickweed: Creativity, dispelling negativity, peace.

Chicory: Attraction, banishing, dispelling negativity, endings, job hunting, overcoming obstacles, power, prosperity, protection, release, reversing, success, transitions, wishes. Egyptians ate chicory as a vegetable.

Chili Peppers and Chili Powder: Banishing, communication, dispelling negativity, endings, overcoming obstacles, protection, purification, release, reversing, transitions.

Chives: Beginnings, communication, creativity, inspiration, magic power, transitions, wishes.

Chocolate: Power, wishes.

Chrysanthemum: Blessing, dispelling negativity, endings, legal matters, magic power, peace, protection, reconciliation, release, reversing, transitions.

Cinnamon (Cassia): Attraction, banishing, beginnings, blessing, communication, creativity, dispelling negativity, endings, inspiration, job hunting, legal matters, magic power, overcoming obstacles, peace, power, prosperity, protection, purification, reconciliation, reversing, success, wishes. Egyptians used it in embalming and as offerings.

Citronella: Attraction, banishing, creativity, dispelling negativity, endings, legal matters, overcoming obstacles, protection, purification, release, reversing, transitions, wishes.

Civet: Magic power, power, protection.

Clary Sage: Attraction, communication, creativity, dispelling negativity, inspiration, overcoming obstacles, peace, protection, purification, reconciliation, wishes.

Clove: Attraction, banishing, blessing, communication, creativity, dispelling negativity, endings, inspiration, legal matters, magic power, overcoming obstacles, peace, power, prosperity, protection, purification, reconciliation, release, reversing, success, wishes.

Clover: Attraction, banishing, beginnings, blessing, dispelling negativity, endings, job hunting, magic power, overcoming obstacles, peace, power, prosperity, protection, purification, release, reversing, success, transitions, wishes.

Coconut: Attraction, banishing, blessing, communication, creativity, endings, inspiration, job hunting, legal matters, overcoming obstacles, peace, prosperity, protection, purification, reversing, success, transitions, wishes.

Coins: Attraction, job hunting, legal matters, prosperity, success, wishes.

Coltsfoot: Banishing, blessing, communication, creativity, dispelling negativity, endings, inspiration, legal matters, overcoming obstacles, peace, power, protection, release, wishes.

Columbine: Overcoming obstacles, power.

Comfrey: Attraction, banishing, blessing, dispelling negativity, endings, job hunting, legal matters, peace, prosperity, protection, release, reversing.

Copal: Banishing, blessing, communication, dispelling negativity, endings, inspiration, magic power, protection, purification, reconciliation, release, reversing, transitions.

Coriander (Cilantro): Attraction, beginnings, blessing, communication, creativity, dispelling negativity, inspiration, job hunting, legal matters, magic power, overcoming obstacles, peace, power, prosperity, protection, reconciliation, release, reversing, success, wishes. Egyptians used it as a funerary offering.

Corn: Attraction, blessing (yellow or blue meal), creativity, inspiration, job hunting, prosperity (yellow), protection (red), purification (blue meal), success, wishes (popcorn).

Crabapple: Magic power.

Crabgrass: Attraction, overcoming obstacles, power.

Cranberry: Dispelling negativity, endings, inspiration, overcoming obstacles, protection, reconciliation, reversing, transitions, wishes. Used to create a magical ink.

Cucumber: Attraction, blessing, communication, creativity, inspiration, job hunting, peace, prosperity, release, success, wishes.

Cumin: Attraction, banishing, blessing, communication, dispelling negativity, endings, job hunting, overcoming obstacles, peace, prosperity, protection, purification, reconciliation, release, reversing, success.

Cyclamen: Blessing, creativity, dispelling negativity, legal matters, peace, protection, reversing, transitions.

Cypress: Banishing, blessing, communication, dispelling negativity, endings, inspiration, legal matters, overcoming obstacles, peace, power, protection, purification, reconciliation, release, reversing, transitions, wishes. Egyptians used cypress for coffins.

Daffodil*: Banishing, beginnings, blessing, creativity, dispelling negativity, endings, protection, purification, reversing, wishes.

Daisy: Blessing, communication, creativity, dispelling negativity, peace, protection, wishes.

Damiana: Communication, inspiration, magic power, peace, purification, reconciliation.

Dandelion: Attraction, beginnings, blessing, communication, creativity, endings, inspiration, magic power, overcoming obstacles, power, protection, release, wishes.

Date: Attraction, banishing, creativity, dispelling negativity, endings, legal matters, overcoming obstacles, peace, power, prosperity, purification. Deity: Isis.

Datura (Jimsonweed)*: Banishing, communication, dispelling negativity, endings, inspiration, legal matters, magic power, protection, purification, reversing, wishes. One of the ingredients in flying ointment.

Devil's Shoestring: Attraction, banishing, blessing, dispelling negativity, endings, job hunting, legal matters, magic power, power, prosperity, protection, purification, reversing, success.

Dill: Attraction, banishing, blessing, communication, creativity, dispelling negativity, endings, inspiration, job hunting, legal matters, magic power, overcoming obstacles, peace, power, prosperity, protection, purification, reconciliation, release, reversing, success.

Dirt: Attraction, banishing, beginnings, blessing, communication, creativity, dispelling negativity, endings, inspiration, job hunting, legal matters, overcoming obstacles, power, prosperity, protection, purification, reconciliation, release, reversing, success, wishes.

Dittany of Crete: Beginnings, communication, creativity, dispelling negativity, endings, inspiration, overcoming obstacles, power, release, transitions. Deity: Osiris.

Dodder: Banishing, communication, dispelling negativity, endings, inspiration, overcoming obstacles, peace, release, reversing, transitions.

Dog Hair (black): Banishing, endings.

Dogwood: Communication, inspiration, overcoming obstacles, power, protection, wishes.

Dragon's Blood: Attraction, banishing, blessing, communication, creativity, dispelling negativity, endings, inspiration, job hunting, legal matters, magic power, overcoming obstacles, peace, power, prosperity, protection, purification, release, reversing, transitions. Used to create a magical ink.

Echinacea: Attraction, job hunting, magic power, overcoming obstacles, power, prosperity, protection, success.

Egg: Banishing, dispelling negativity, purification, release.

Egg Shells (powdered): Protection, purification.

Elder*: Attraction, banishing, beginnings, blessing, communication, creativity, dispelling negativity, endings, inspiration, job hunting, legal matters, magic power, peace, power, prosperity, protection, purification, release, reversing, success, transitions, wishes. The seeds are poisonous.

Elecampane: Banishing, blessing, communication, creativity, dispelling negativity, endings, inspiration, magic power, protection, purification, transitions.

Elm: Communication, creativity, endings, inspiration, protection, release, transitions.

Endive: Attraction, beginnings, communication, creativity, dispelling negativity, inspiration, magic power, overcoming obstacles, power, prosperity, reconciliation, release, reversing, success, transitions.

Eucalyptus: Banishing, beginnings, blessing, creativity, dispelling negativity, endings, inspiration, legal matters, magic power, overcoming obstacles, peace, power, protection, purification, reconciliation, release, reversing, wishes. Used to break bad habits.

Eyebright: Banishing, beginnings, blessing, communication, creativity, dispelling negativity, endings, inspiration, magic power, overcoming obstacles, peace, purification, reconciliation, release, reversing, transitions.

Feathers: Communication.

Feathers (turkey): Attraction, job hunting, protection, reversing, success.

Fennel: Attraction, banishing, blessing, communication, creativity, dispelling negativity, endings, inspiration, job hunting, legal matters, magic power, overcoming obstacles, power, prosperity, protection, purification, release, reversing, success, transitions.

Fenugreek: Attraction, communication, creativity, dispelling negativity, inspiration, magic power, overcoming obstacles, prosperity, protection, reconciliation, reversing, success, transitions.

Feverfew: Protection, purification.

Fig: Attraction, blessing, communication, creativity, inspiration, job hunting, legal matters, overcoming obstacles, peace, power, prosperity, protection, reversing, success. Deity: Isis.

Figwort: Dispelling negativity, peace, protection, reversing.

Fingernail Clippings: Banishing, blessing, endings, magic power, reconciliation, reversing, wishes. Used in sympathetic magic to represent the person you wish to influence.

Fir: Attraction, banishing, beginnings, communication, creativity, dispelling negativity, endings, inspiration, job hunting, overcoming obstacles, peace, power, prosperity, protection, purification, release, success, transitions.

Five-finger Grass (Cinquefoil): Attraction, banishing, blessing, communication, creativity, dispelling negativity, endings, inspiration, job hunting, legal matters, magic power, peace, power, prosperity, protection, purification, reversing, success, wishes. One of the ingredients in flying ointment.

Flax (Linseed): Attraction, banishing, blessing, communication, dispelling negativity, endings, inspiration, job hunting, overcoming obstacles, power, prosperity, protection, purification, release, reversing, success, transitions.

Foxglove*: Communication, inspiration, magic power, power, protection.

Frangipani (Plumeria)*: Attraction.

Frankincense: Attraction, banishing, blessing, communication, creativity, dispelling negativity, endings, inspiration, job hunting, legal matters, magic power, overcoming obstacles, peace, power, prosperity, protection, purification, release, reversing, success, transitions, wishes. Egyptians used this in the making of kohl, the distinctive black eye makeup. Frankincense was burned at sunset to honor Ra. Deities: Isis, Ra.

Freesia: Beginnings, dispelling negativity, overcoming obstacles, peace, release.

Fumitory*: Attraction, banishing, beginnings, blessing, dispelling negativity, endings, job hunting, overcoming obstacles, prosperity, protection, purification, release, reversing, transitions.

Galangal: Attraction, banishing, blessing, communication, dispelling negativity, endings, inspiration, job hunting, legal matters, magic power, overcoming obstacles, power, prosperity, protection, purification, release, reversing, success. Used to break bad habits.

Galbanum: Inspiration, peace, purification.

Gardenia: Communication, inspiration, peace, power, prosperity, reversing.

Garlic: Attraction, banishing, communication, dispelling negativity, endings, job hunting, legal matters, magic power, overcoming obstacles, power, prosperity, protection, purification, release, reversing, success, wishes. Egyptians used garlic as a form of monetary exchange and as an aphrodisiac.

Gentian: Banishing, creativity, dispelling negativity, endings, magic power, overcoming obstacles, peace, power, protection, reconciliation, release, reversing, transitions.

Geranium: Attraction, banishing, communication, creativity, dispelling negativity, endings, legal matters, overcoming obstacles, peace, prosperity, protection, purification, reversing, success.

Ginger: Attraction, blessing, communication, inspiration, job hunting, magic power, overcoming obstacles, power, prosperity, protection, purification, reversing, success.

Ginseng: Attraction, banishing, beginnings, blessing, communication, creativity, dispelling negativity, endings, inspiration, job hunting, magic power, overcoming obstacles, power, prosperity, protection, purification, reversing, success, wishes. May be used as a substitute for mandrake.

Grains of Paradise: Attraction, blessing, communication, creativity, dispelling negativity, inspiration, job hunting, overcoming obstacles, power, prosperity, protection, reversing, success, wishes.

Grape: Attraction, communication, creativity, inspiration, job hunting, magic power, peace, power, prosperity, success, transitions. Used to create a magical ink.

Grapefruit: Banishing, dispelling negativity, endings, peace, protection, purification, reversing.

Graveyard Dirt: Cursing, hexing. It is best to leave an offering on the grave to "pay" for what you took.

Gum Mastic: Banishing, blessing, communication, creativity, dispelling negativity, endings, inspiration, legal matters, magic power, overcoming obstacles, protection, purification, release, reversing, transitions, wishes.

Hail: Legal matters, reconciliation, reversing.

Hair: Magic power, wishes. Used in sympathetic magic to represent the person you wish to influence.

Handwriting Sample: Used in sympathetic magic to represent the person you wish to influence.

Hawthorn: Attraction, blessing, communication, creativity, dispelling negativity, inspiration, job hunting, magic power, peace, power, prosperity, protection, purification, success, wishes.

Hazel: Attraction, beginnings, blessing, communication, creativity, inspiration, magic power, overcoming obstacles, power, protection, reconciliation, reversing, wishes.

Heather: Banishing, blessing, dispelling negativity, magic power, overcoming obstacles, peace, protection, purification, transitions, wishes. Deities: Isis, Osiris.

Heliotrope*: Attraction, banishing, blessing, communication, dispelling negativity, endings, inspiration, job hunting, overcoming obstacles, peace, prosperity, release, reversing, success.

Hemlock*: Banishing, beginnings, blessing, creativity, dispelling negativity, endings, inspiration, legal matters, magic power, overcoming obstacles, power, protection, purification, release, transitions.

Hemp: Communication, creativity, inspiration, magic power, peace, release, transitions. One of the ingredients in flying ointment.

Henbane*: Banishing, blessing, communication, dispelling negativity, endings, inspiration, magic power, protection, purification. One of the ingredients in flying ointment.

Henna: Attraction, beginnings, communication, job hunting, magic power, peace, prosperity, protection, success.

Hibiscus: Blessing, communication, dispelling negativity, inspiration, peace, power, reconciliation, wishes.

Hickory: Attraction, banishing, communication, dispelling negativity, endings, job hunting, legal matters, overcoming obstacles, peace, prosperity, protection, reconciliation, reversing, success, wishes.

High John the Conqueror (Jalap)*: Attraction, banishing, blessing, communication, dispelling negativity, endings, inspiration, job hunting, legal matters, magic power, overcoming obstacles, peace, power, prosperity, protection, purification, reversing, success, wishes.

Holly: Banishing, beginnings, blessing, communication, dispelling negativity, endings, legal matters, magic power, overcoming obstacles, power, protection, purification, release, reversing, transitions, wishes. The berries are poisonous.

Hollyhock: Attraction, banishing, communication, dispelling negativity, endings, inspiration, job hunting, overcoming obstacles, peace, prosperity, protection, reversing, success.

Honey: Attraction, blessing, creativity, job hunting, legal matters, peace, prosperity, purification, success, wishes.

Honeydew: Reconciliation.

Honeysuckle: Attraction, beginnings, blessing, communication, creativity, endings, inspiration, job hunting, legal matters, peace, power, prosperity, protection, reversing, success, transitions.

Hops: Communication, creativity, inspiration, legal matters, peace, protection, purification.

Horehound: Banishing, blessing, communication, creativity, dispelling negativity, endings, inspiration, overcoming obstacles, power, protection, release, reversing, transitions. Deities: Horus, Isis, Osiris.

Houseleek: Banishing, dispelling negativity, endings, protection, reversing.

Huckleberry: Attraction, banishing, blessing, dispelling negativity, endings, inspiration, job hunting, overcoming obstacles, prosperity, protection, purification, reversing, success, wishes.

Hyacinth: Blessing, dispelling negativity, endings, peace, protection, purification, release, transitions.

Hydrangea: Banishing, dispelling negativity, endings, job hunting, protection, purification, reversing.

Hyssop: Attraction, banishing, blessing, communication, creativity, dispelling negativity, endings, job hunting, legal matters, overcoming obstacles, peace, prosperity, protection, purification, reconciliation, release, reversing.

Ice (Snow): Attraction, banishing, communication, creativity, endings, inspiration, job hunting, legal matters, overcoming obstacles, prosperity, protection, reconciliation, release, reversing, success, transitions, wishes. Used to "freeze" or stop someone or something.

Iris: Attraction, beginnings, blessing, creativity, endings, inspiration, job hunting, magic power, overcoming obstacles, peace, power, prosperity, protection, purification, reconciliation, release, success, transitions.

Irish Moss: Attraction, blessing, job hunting, overcoming obstacles, prosperity, protection, reversing, success.

Ivy*: Attraction, beginnings, blessing, communication, creativity, dispelling negativity, inspiration, job hunting, magic power, overcoming obstacles, peace, power, prosperity, protection, success, transitions, wishes. Deity: Osiris.

Jasmine*: Attraction, banishing, blessing, communication, creativity, dispelling negativity, inspiration, job hunting, legal matters, peace, power, prosperity, protection, purification, reversing, success, wishes. The berries are poisonous.

Job's Tears: Attraction, blessing, job hunting, magic power, overcoming obstacles, prosperity, reversing, success, wishes.

Juniper: Attraction, banishing, blessing, communication, creativity, dispelling negativity, endings, inspiration, job hunting, overcoming obstacles, peace, power, prosperity, protection, purification, release, reversing, success, transitions, wishes.

Labdanum: Communication, creativity, dispelling negativity, inspiration, overcoming obstacles, purification, transitions.

Lady's Mantle: Blessing, magic power, overcoming obstacles, peace, transitions, wishes.

Larkspur*: Banishing, dispelling negativity, endings, protection, purification.

Lavender: Attraction, banishing, beginnings, blessing, communication, creativity, dispelling negativity, endings, inspiration, job hunting, legal matters, magic power, overcoming obstacles, peace, power, prosperity, protection, purification, reconciliation, release, reversing, success, transitions, wishes.

Lemon: Blessing, communication, dispelling negativity, inspiration, legal matters, magic power, peace, power, protection, purification, reversing. Used to "sour" a habit or relationship.

Lemon Balm (Melissa): Attraction, communication, creativity, dispelling negativity, endings, inspiration, job hunting, legal matters, overcoming obstacles, peace, power, prosperity, purification, reconciliation, release, success, wishes.

Lemon Verbena: Attraction, banishing, dispelling negativity, endings, magic power, overcoming obstacles, peace, power, prosperity, protection, purification, reconciliation, reversing, success, wishes.

Lemongrass: Beginnings, blessing, communication, dispelling negativity, inspiration, legal matters, peace, power, protection, purification, reversing, wishes.

Lettuce: Attraction, communication, creativity, inspiration, job hunting, overcoming obstacles, prosperity, protection, success, wishes. Deity: Min.

Licorice: Communication, overcoming obstacles, peace, power, protection, reconciliation, wishes.

Lilac: Attraction, banishing, communication, creativity, dispelling negativity, endings, inspiration, job hunting, legal matters, peace, power, prosperity, protection, purification, reconciliation, release, reversing.

Lily: Banishing, beginnings, communication, creativity, dispelling negativity, endings, overcoming obstacles, peace, power, protection, purification, release, reversing, transitions. Deity: Nephthys.

Lily of the Valley*: Blessing, dispelling negativity, inspiration, magic power, peace, protection, reversing.

Lime: Banishing, creativity, dispelling negativity, endings, magic power, overcoming obstacles, power, protection, purification, release.

Linden: Attraction, blessing, communication, endings, inspiration, legal matters, overcoming obstacles, peace, power, protection, reconciliation, reversing, success, transitions, wishes.

Lobelia*: Power, wishes.

Loosestrife: Dispelling negativity, overcoming obstacles, peace, power, protection, purification, reconciliation, release.

Lotus: Beginnings, blessing, communication, creativity, dispelling negativity, endings, inspiration, legal matters, magic power, overcoming obstacles, peace, power, protection, purification, release, reversing, success, transitions, wishes. Egyptian symbol of life and creation. As a sacred plant, it was used as an offering to the gods. Deities: Horus, Isis, Nefertem, Osiris.

Lovage: Attraction, beginnings, dispelling negativity, job hunting, legal matters, power, prosperity, protection, purification, success.

Lucky Hand Root (Salep): Attraction, banishing, beginnings, blessing, dispelling negativity, endings, job hunting, magic power, prosperity, protection, reversing, success, wishes.

Lupine: Communication, creativity, endings, inspiration, transitions.

Mace: Attraction, blessing, communication, creativity, inspiration, job hunting, overcoming obstacles, prosperity, protection, success.

Magnolia: Banishing, dispelling negativity, inspiration, peace, purification, wishes.

Maidenhair Fern: Peace, purification, reconciliation.

Male Fern: Attraction, banishing, blessing, dispelling negativity, endings, job hunting, magic power, overcoming obstacles, power, prosperity, protection, purification, release, success.

Mandrake*: Attraction, banishing, beginnings, blessing, communication, creativity, dispelling negativity, endings, inspiration, job hunting, magic power, overcoming obstacles, power, prosperity, protection, purification, release, reversing, success, transitions, wishes. One of the ingredients in flying ointment. Deity: Hathor.

Mango: Banishing, endings, power, protection, release, reversing, wishes.

Maple: Attraction, blessing, communication, creativity, inspiration, job hunting, legal matters, peace, power, prosperity, reversing, success, wishes. This applies to the syrup as well.

Marigold (Calendula): Attraction, banishing, beginnings, blessing, communication, creativity, dispelling negativity, endings, inspiration, job hunting, legal matters, overcoming obstacles, peace, power, prosperity, protection, purification, reconciliation, release, reversing, success, wishes.

Marjoram: Attraction, banishing, beginnings, blessing, communication, dispelling negativity, endings, inspiration, job hunting, peace, prosperity, protection, purification, reconciliation, release, success, transitions, wishes.

Marshmallow: Banishing, beginnings, blessing, communication, creativity, dispelling negativity, endings, inspiration, overcoming obstacles, peace, protection, reconciliation, reversing, wishes.

Meadowsweet: Attraction, beginnings, blessing, communication, dispelling negativity, inspiration, job hunting, legal matters, peace, prosperity, protection, reconciliation, reversing, transitions.

Mesquite: Banishing, dispelling negativity, magic power, purification.

Milk (coconut): Dispelling negativity, protection, purification.

Milk (cow): Prosperity, protection. Used to create an invisible magical ink. Deity: Hathor.

Milk (goat): Legal matters, power, success.

Milk (soy): Job hunting, success.

Milkweed: Beginnings, blessing, creativity, inspiration, magic power, overcoming obstacles, protection, transitions.

Mimosa: Banishing, blessing, creativity, dispelling negativity, endings, inspiration, magic power, peace, protection, purification, reversing, wishes.

Mistletoe*: Attraction, banishing, beginnings, blessing, communication, creativity, dispelling negativity, endings, inspiration, job hunting, magic power, overcoming obstacles, peace, power, prosperity, protection, purification, reconciliation, release, reversing, success, transitions, wishes. The berries are poisonous.

Molasses: Attraction, blessing, legal matters, overcoming obstacles, peace, power, prosperity, success. Used in a spell bottle to keep someone "stuck" in a situation.

Moneywort: Attraction, blessing, job hunting, overcoming obstacles, prosperity, success, transitions, wishes.

Moonwort: Attraction, banishing, communication, creativity, inspiration, job hunting, overcoming obstacles, prosperity, release, reversing, success.

Motherwort: Creativity, dispelling negativity, endings, inspiration, overcoming obstacles, peace, power, protection, reconciliation, release, reversing, success, transitions, wishes.

Mugwort: Banishing, blessing, communication, creativity, dispelling negativity, endings, inspiration, magic power, overcoming obstacles, peace, power, protection, purification, reconciliation, release, reversing, wishes.

Mulberry: Communication, creativity, inspiration, legal matters, magic power, overcoming obstacles, power, protection, release, success, wishes.

Mullein*: Banishing, communication, dispelling negativity, endings, inspiration, legal matters, magic power, overcoming obstacles, peace, power, protection, purification, release, reversing. Used as a substitute for graveyard dirt.

Musk: Attraction, blessing, creativity, dispelling negativity, magic power, overcoming obstacles, power, prosperity, purification, reconciliation, success, wishes.

Mustard: Attraction, banishing, blessing, communication, creativity, dispelling negativity, endings, inspiration, job hunting, legal matters, overcoming obstacles, power, prosperity, protection, purification, reversing, success. Black mustard seed is used to confuse and white mustard seed is used for protection.

Myrrh: Attraction, banishing, beginnings, blessing, communication, dispelling negativity, endings, inspiration, legal matters, magic power, overcoming obstacles, peace, power, prosperity, protection, purification, reconciliation, release, reversing, success, transitions, wishes. Egyptians used this in embalming. Myrrh was burned at noon to honor Ra and was used in the temples of Isis. Deities: Isis, Ra.

Myrtle: Attraction, banishing, beginnings, blessing, communication, creativity, dispelling negativity, endings, inspiration, job hunting, legal matters, magic power, overcoming obstacles, peace, power, prosperity, protection, release, reversing, transitions. Used to ward off abuse and violence. Deity: Hathor.

Nails (Rusty or Iron): Banishing, dispelling negativity, protection, reversing. Used as an ingredient in oils and spell bottles.

Narcissus*: Banishing, communication, creativity, dispelling negativity, endings, inspiration, peace, release, reversing, transitions. Deity: Isis.

Neroli: Beginnings, blessing, creativity, job hunting, overcoming obstacles, peace, prosperity, success, transitions, wishes.

Nettle: Banishing, blessing, dispelling negativity, endings, legal matters, magic power, overcoming obstacles, peace, power, protection, purification, reversing.

Nutmeg: Attraction, blessing, communication, creativity, inspiration, job hunting, legal matters, peace, power, prosperity, protection, reversing, success, wishes.

Oak: Attraction, beginnings, blessing, communication, creativity, dispelling negativity, endings, inspiration, job hunting, magic power, overcoming obstacles, power, prosperity, protection, purification, release, reversing, success, transitions. Deity: Shu.

Oakmoss: Attraction, banishing, blessing, communication, dispelling negativity, endings, inspiration, job hunting, magic power, prosperity, protection, reversing, success.

Oat: Attraction, job hunting, prosperity, success.

Oleander*: Banishing, dispelling negativity, endings, peace, release, transitions. Deity: Osiris.

Olive: Attraction, blessing, communication, creativity, dispelling negativity, inspiration, job hunting, legal matters, overcoming obstacles, peace, power, prosperity, protection, purification, success. Deity: Ra.

Onion: Blessing, peace, power (purple or red onion), attraction, banishing, communication, dispelling negativity, endings, magic power, overcoming obstacles, prosperity, protection, purification, reconciliation, release, reversing, success.

Orange: Attraction, beginnings, blessing, communication, creativity, dispelling negativity, inspiration, job hunting, legal matters, overcoming obstacles, peace, prosperity, purification, success, transitions, wishes.

Orchid: Attraction, beginnings, blessing, communication, creativity, inspiration, job hunting, magic power, peace, power, prosperity, success, wishes.

Oregano: Attraction, banishing, blessing, communication, creativity, dispelling negativity, inspiration, job hunting, legal matters, magic power, overcoming obstacles, peace, power, prosperity, protection, reconciliation, reversing, success, wishes.

Orris: Attraction, banishing, beginnings, blessing, communication, creativity, dispelling negativity, endings, inspiration, overcoming obstacles, peace, power, protection, purification, reversing, transitions. Deities: Isis, Osiris.

Palm: Attraction, beginnings, blessing, communication, creativity, inspiration, peace, power, prosperity, protection, purification, transitions. Deities: Isis, Thoth.

Pansy: Blessing, communication, endings, inspiration, legal matters, protection.

Papaya: Attraction, job hunting, magic power, prosperity, protection, reversing, success, wishes.

Parsley: Attraction, banishing, blessing, communication, creativity, dispelling negativity, endings, job hunting, magic power, overcoming obstacles, peace, power, prosperity, protection, purification, release, success, transitions, wishes.

Passionflower: Blessing, communication, dispelling negativity, overcoming obstacles, peace, protection, purification, reconciliation, reversing, transitions, wishes.

Patchouli: Attraction, banishing, beginnings, blessing, communication, creativity, dispelling negativity, endings, inspiration, job hunting, legal matters, magic power, overcoming obstacles, peace, power, prosperity, protection, purification, reconciliation, release, reversing, success, transitions, wishes. Used as a substitute for graveyard dirt.

Peach: Attraction, banishing, blessing, creativity, dispelling negativity, endings, inspiration, legal matters, overcoming obstacles, peace, power, prosperity, protection, release, reversing, success, transitions, wishes.

Pear: Beginnings, blessing, overcoming obstacles, power, protection.

Pecan: Attraction, beginnings, blessing, job hunting, prosperity, success.

Pennyroyal: Attraction, banishing, beginnings, blessing, communication, dispelling negativity, endings, legal matters, overcoming obstacles, peace, power, prosperity, protection, purification, reconciliation, release, reversing, success, transitions. Do not take internally or use if pregnant.

Peony*: Attraction, banishing, blessing, dispelling negativity, endings, job hunting, magic power, overcoming obstacles, power, prosperity, protection, purification, release, reversing, success.

Peppermint: Attraction, banishing, beginnings, blessing, communication, creativity, dispelling negativity, endings, inspiration, job hunting, legal matters, magic power, peace, power, prosperity, protection, purification, release, reversing, success, transitions.

Periwinkle*: Attraction, banishing, dispelling negativity, endings, magic power, overcoming obstacles, peace, prosperity, protection, release, reversing, transitions, wishes.

Photographs: Used in sympathetic magic to represent the person you wish to influence.

Pimpernel: Banishing, blessing, dispelling negativity, overcoming obstacles, prosperity, protection, purification, release, reversing, transitions.

Pine: Attraction, banishing, beginnings, blessing, communication, creativity, dispelling negativity, endings, inspiration, job hunting, legal matters, magic power, overcoming obstacles, peace, power, prosperity, protection, purification, release, reversing, success, transitions. Deity: Osiris.

Pineapple: Attraction, beginnings, blessing, creativity, inspiration, job hunting, peace, power, prosperity, success.

Pins and Needles: Attraction, job hunting, magic power, prosperity, protection, release, success. Used as an ingredient in oils and spell bottles.

Plum: Dispelling negativity, protection, reversing.

Poke (Poke Root)*: Banishing, dispelling negativity, endings, legal matters, overcoming obstacles, power, purification, reversing.

Pomegranate: Attraction, beginnings, blessing, communication, creativity, endings, inspiration, job hunting, magic power, overcoming obstacles, prosperity, protection, success, transitions, wishes. Used to create a magical ink or as a substitute for blood.

Poplar: Attraction, communication, creativity, dispelling negativity, endings, inspiration, job hunting, overcoming obstacles, power, prosperity, protection, release, success, transitions, wishes. One of the ingredients in flying ointment.

Poppet (Doll): Used in sympathetic magic to represent the person you wish to influence.

Poppy: Attraction, blessing, communication, creativity, inspiration, job hunting, legal matters, magic power, peace, power, prosperity, reconciliation, success, wishes. Use the seeds to confuse.

Primrose (Cowslip): Attraction, beginnings, creativity, dispelling negativity, inspiration, job hunting, magic power, overcoming obstacles, peace, power, prosperity, protection, reconciliation, success, transitions.

Pumpkin: Attraction, blessing, creativity, job hunting, prosperity, success, wishes.

Purslane: Attraction, banishing, blessing, communication, dispelling negativity, endings, job hunting, overcoming obstacles, peace, prosperity, protection, purification, reversing, success, transitions.

Quince: Banishing, beginnings, blessing, communication, dispelling negativity, peace, protection, reconciliation, reversing.

Raspberry: Banishing, dispelling negativity, overcoming obstacles, power, protection, release, reversing, transitions. Used to create a magical ink.

Rice: Attraction, beginnings, blessing, creativity, prosperity, protection, success, wishes.

Rose: Banishing, beginnings, blessing, communication, creativity, dispelling negativity, endings, inspiration, legal matters, magic power, overcoming obstacles, peace, power, protection, purification, reconciliation, release, transitions, wishes. Thorns can be used to carve candles and as an ingredient in oils and spell bottles. Deities: Hathor, Isis.

Rosemary: Attraction, banishing, beginnings, blessing, communication, creativity, dispelling negativity, endings, inspiration, job hunting, legal matters, magic power, overcoming obstacles, peace, power, prosperity, protection, purification, reconciliation, release, reversing, success, transitions.

Rowan: Banishing, blessing, communication, creativity, dispelling negativity, inspiration, magic power, overcoming obstacles, peace, power, prosperity, protection, purification, reconciliation, release, reversing, success, transitions.

Rue*: Attraction, banishing, blessing, communication, creativity, dispelling negativity, endings, inspiration, job hunting, magic power, overcoming obstacles, peace, power, prosperity, protection, purification, reconciliation, release, reversing, success, wishes.

Safflower: Banishing, communication, dispelling negativity, endings, magic power, power, reversing.

Saffron: Attraction, blessing, communication, creativity, dispelling negativity, inspiration, job hunting, overcoming obstacles, peace, power, prosperity, reversing, success, wishes.

Sage: Attraction, banishing, beginnings, blessing, communication, creativity, dispelling negativity, endings, inspiration, job hunting, legal matters, magic power, overcoming obstacles, peace, power, prosperity, protection, purification, reconciliation, release, reversing, success, transitions, wishes.

St. John's Wort*: Banishing, blessing, communication, creativity, dispelling negativity, endings, inspiration, legal matters, magic power, overcoming obstacles, peace, power, prosperity, protection, purification, release, reversing, success.

Saliva: Used in sympathetic magic to represent the person you wish to influence.

Salt: Attraction, banishing, blessing, dispelling negativity, endings, job hunting, overcoming obstacles, prosperity, protection, purification, reversing, success, transitions. Black salt (colored black or mixed with black pepper) is often called for in cursing and hexing spells.

Sandalwood: Attraction, banishing, beginnings, blessing, communication, creativity, dispelling negativity, endings, inspiration, job hunting, legal matters, magic power, overcoming obstacles, peace, power, prosperity, protection, purification, reconciliation, release, reversing, success, transitions, wishes. Deity: Isis.

Sarsaparilla: Attraction, blessing, communication, creativity, inspiration, job hunting, overcoming obstacles, power, prosperity, protection, success.

Sassafras: Attraction, banishing, blessing, job hunting, legal matters, peace, power, prosperity, protection, reversing, success.

Savory: Creativity, peace.

Scullcap: Attraction, beginnings, blessing, creativity, magic power, peace, prosperity, protection.

Senna: Banishing, communication, creativity, endings, inspiration, legal matters, overcoming obstacles, reconciliation, release.

Sesame: Attraction, banishing, blessing, dispelling negativity, endings, job hunting, overcoming obstacles, prosperity, protection, purification, release, success, transitions.

Sexual Fluids: Used in sympathetic magic to represent the person you wish to influence.

Slippery Elm: Banishing, communication, creativity, dispelling negativity, endings, inspiration, magic power, peace, power, protection, reconciliation, release, reversing.

Snapdragon: Banishing, blessing, communication, creativity, dispelling negativity, endings, inspiration, overcoming obstacles, prosperity, protection, purification, reversing.

Solomon's Seal: Attraction, banishing, blessing, communication, creativity, dispelling negativity, endings, inspiration, job hunting, legal matters, overcoming obstacles, power, prosperity, protection, purification, reversing, success.

Southernwood: Banishing, beginnings, blessing, communication, dispelling negativity, endings, magic power, overcoming obstacles, peace, power, protection, purification, reconciliation, reversing, transitions, wishes.

Spanish Moss: Attraction, beginnings, blessing, creativity, dispelling negativity, inspiration, job hunting, prosperity, protection, success.

Spearmint: Attraction, banishing, beginnings, blessing, communication, creativity, dispelling negativity, endings, inspiration, job hunting, legal matters, overcoming obstacles, peace, prosperity, protection, purification, release, reversing, success, transitions, wishes.

Spikenard: Attraction, banishing, blessing, communication, creativity, dispelling negativity, inspiration, job hunting, legal matters, overcoming obstacles, peace, power, prosperity, protection, purification, reconciliation, release, reversing, transitions.

Star Anise: Attraction, banishing, beginnings, blessing, communication, creativity, dispelling negativity, endings, inspiration, job hunting, legal matters, peace, power, prosperity, protection, purification, success.

Storax: Banishing, beginnings, communication, creativity, dispelling negativity, endings, inspiration, magic power, overcoming obstacles, power, prosperity, protection, purification, reconciliation, release, reversing, success, transitions, wishes. Deity: Thoth.

Strawberry: Attraction, beginnings, blessing, communication, creativity, inspiration, job hunting, peace, prosperity, success. Used to create a magical ink.

Sulfur: Banishing, dispelling negativity, endings, legal matters, magic power, overcoming obstacles, power, protection, purification, release, reversing, transitions. Has a foul odor when burned.

Sunflower: Attraction, banishing, blessing, communication, creativity, dispelling negativity, endings, inspiration, job hunting, magic power, overcoming obstacles, peace, power, prosperity, protection, reconciliation, release, reversing, success, transitions, wishes.

Sweat: Used in sympathetic magic to represent the person you wish to influence.

Sweet Pea: Attraction, blessing, overcoming obstacles, peace, power, reversing.

Sweetgrass: Banishing, dispelling negativity, protection, purification.

Sycamore: Blessing, communication, endings, overcoming obstacles, power, reconciliation, release, transitions. Deity: Hathor.

Tamarisk: Banishing, blessing, dispelling negativity, endings, overcoming obstacles, protection, purification, release, reversing.

Tangerine: Attraction, dispelling negativity, inspiration, magic power, peace, protection, purification, wishes.

Tansy*: Banishing, blessing, creativity, dispelling negativity, endings, inspiration, legal matters, overcoming obstacles, power, protection, purification, release, reversing, transitions, wishes.

Tarragon: Attraction, communication, creativity, dispelling negativity, endings, inspiration, job hunting, legal matters, overcoming obstacles, power, prosperity, protection, release, reversing, success, transitions, wishes.

Tea: Attraction, communication, inspiration, job hunting, overcoming obstacles, power, prosperity, protection (black tea), success, wishes (green tea).

Tea Tree: Banishing, communication, creativity, dispelling negativity, inspiration, overcoming obstacles, peace, purification, reconciliation, release.

Teak: Communication, overcoming obstacles, peace, power, prosperity, release, transitions.

Thistle: Banishing, dispelling negativity, endings, overcoming obstacles, power, protection, purification, release, reversing.

Thorns: Used to carve candles or as an ingredient in oils and spell bottles.

Thyme: Attraction, banishing, beginnings, blessing, communication, creativity, dispelling negativity, endings, inspiration, job hunting, legal matters, magic power, overcoming obstacles, peace, power, prosperity, protection, purification, reconciliation, release, reversing, success, transitions, wishes.

Tinfoil: Magnifies the power of any spell. Used in spell packets and mojo bags with the reflective side facing out.

Tobacco*: Attraction, banishing, beginnings, blessing, communication, creativity, dispelling negativity, endings, inspiration, job hunting, legal matters, magic power, overcoming obstacles, power, prosperity, protection, purification, release, reversing, success, transitions. Used as a substitute for sulfur or any poisonous herb.

Tomato: Attraction, banishing, dispelling negativity, endings, prosperity, protection, reversing.

Tonka Bean*: Attraction, blessing, job hunting, overcoming obstacles, power, prosperity, reversing, success, wishes.

Tuberose: Communication, dispelling negativity, inspiration, legal matters, overcoming obstacles, peace, protection, release, transitions.

Tulip: Attraction, beginnings, blessing, job hunting, power, prosperity, protection, purification, success.

Turmeric (Goldenseal): Banishing, blessing, dispelling negativity, endings, magic power, overcoming obstacles, power, prosperity, protection, purification, reversing, success.

Urine: Used as a noxious liquid in spell bottles.

Valerian: Banishing, blessing, communication, creativity, dispelling negativity, endings, magic power, overcoming obstacles, peace, power, prosperity, protection, purification, reconciliation, release, reversing, transitions. Has quite a foul odor. May be used as a substitute for graveyard dirt.

Vanilla: Blessing, inspiration, magic power, peace, power, success.

Vervain: Attraction, banishing, beginnings, blessing, communication, creativity, dispelling negativity, endings, inspiration, job hunting, legal matters, magic power, overcoming obstacles, peace, power, prosperity, protection, purification, reconciliation, release, reversing, success, transitions, wishes. Deity: Isis.

Vetivert: Attraction, banishing, blessing, dispelling negativity, endings, job hunting, legal matters, magic power, overcoming obstacles, peace, power, prosperity, protection, reversing, success.

Vinegar: Banishing, dispelling negativity, endings, overcoming obstacles, protection, purification, release, reversing. Used in oils and spell bottles to "sour" a bad habit or relationship.

Violet: Attraction, banishing, blessing, communication, creativity, endings, inspiration, job hunting, legal matters, overcoming obstacles, peace, prosperity, protection, purification, reconciliation, release, success, transitions, wishes.

Walnut: Attraction, blessing, communication, creativity, magic power, prosperity, wishes.

Water Lily: Beginnings, blessing, communication, creativity, endings, legal matters, peace, protection, purification, release, success, transitions. Egyptian symbol of life and creation. This is most likely the "lotus" of ancient Egypt. Deities: Horus, Isis, Nefertem, Osiris.

Wheat: Attraction, blessing, creativity, job hunting, prosperity, success, transitions, wishes.

Willow: Banishing, communication, creativity, dispelling negativity, endings, inspiration, legal matters, magic power, overcoming obstacles, peace, power, protection, purification, reconciliation, release, reversing, transitions, wishes.

Wintergreen: Attraction, banishing, blessing, communication, dispelling negativity, endings, job hunting, legal matters, overcoming obstacles, power, prosperity, protection, purification, reversing, success.

Wisteria: Attraction, blessing, communication, creativity, inspiration, peace, power, prosperity, protection, release, reversing.

Witch Grass (Couch Grass): Banishing, dispelling negativity, endings, magic power, peace, release, reversing.

Witch Hazel: Banishing, communication, creativity, dispelling negativity, inspiration, magic power, overcoming obstacles, protection, purification, reversing, transitions.

Wood Aloe: Attraction, banishing, blessing, communication, dispelling negativity, magic power, prosperity, protection, purification.

Wood Betony: Banishing, communication, dispelling negativity, endings, inspiration, magic power, overcoming obstacles, power, protection, purification, reconciliation, release, reversing.

Wood Sorrel: Attraction, blessing, dispelling negativity, job hunting, magic power, overcoming obstacles, peace, power, prosperity, protection, purification, release, reversing, success, transitions.

Woodruff: Attraction, banishing, beginnings, blessing, communication, dispelling negativity, endings, inspiration, job hunting, legal matters, magic power, overcoming obstacles, power, prosperity, protection, purification, release, success, transitions.

Wormwood*: Banishing, communication, creativity, dispelling negativity, endings, inspiration, magic power, overcoming obstacles, peace, power, protection, purification, reconciliation, release, reversing, transitions, wishes. Has a foul order. Produces a poisonous smoke when burned.

Yarrow: Banishing, beginnings, blessing, communication, creativity, dispelling negativity, endings, inspiration, legal matters, magic power, overcoming obstacles, peace, power, protection, purification, reconciliation, release, reversing, success, transitions, wishes.

Yellow Dock: Attraction, blessing, creativity, legal matters, prosperity, protection, success.

Yew*: Banishing, beginnings, communication, endings, inspiration, magic power, protection, release, transitions.

Ylang-ylang (Cananga): Attraction, blessing, communication, dispelling negativity, job hunting, legal matters, magic power, overcoming obstacles, peace, power, prosperity, reconciliation, success, wishes.

Yohimbe*: Magic power, power, release.

APPENDIX B

Resources for Spellcasting Materials

Ancient Ways
4075 Telegraph Avenue
Oakland, CA 94609
(510) 653-3244
www.ancientways.com

Artemisia Botanicals
102 Wharf Street
Salem, MA 01970
(978) 745-0065
www.artemisiabotanicals.com

AzureGreen
16 Bell Road, P. O. Box 48
Middlefield, MA 01243-0048
(413) 623-2155
www.azuregreen.com

Ceridwen's Magickal & New Age Supplies
630 South Huttig
Independence, MO 64053
(816) 461-7773

The Crystal Cauldron
360 South Thomas Street
Pomona, CA 91766
(909) 620-9565
www.willowscrystalcauldron.com

Earth Spirits
407 Main Street
Sturbridge, MA 01566
(508) 347-1180
www.earthspirits-herbals.com

Lucky Mojo Curio Company
6632 Covey Road
Forestville, CA 95436
(707) 887-1521
www.luckymojo.com

A Magickal Moon
1717 East Broadway Road
Tempe, AZ 85282
(480) 303-8368

Magus Books & Herbs
1309 ½ 4th Street SE
Minneapolis, MN 55414
(612) 379-7669
www.magusbooks.com

Mystic Valley
3212 Laclede Station Road
St. Louis, MO 63143
(314) 645-3336

Original Products Botanica
2486-88 Webster Avenue
Bronx, NY 10458
(718) 367-9589
www.originalprodcorp.com

Quintessential Oils
847 35th Street
Richmond, CA 94805
(510) 215-2750
www.quintoils.com

Some Enchanted Evening
243 Main Street (Route 9)
Spencer, MA 01562
(508) 885-2050
www.someenchantedevening.us

Taproot Book Store
1200 West Boylston Street
Worcester, MA 01606-1166
(508) 853-5083

Whispered Prayers
1112 Main Street
Manteca, CA 95336
(209) 840-3500
www.whisperedprayers.net

Note: To find all kinds of "witchy" items, you can use the following search engines and websites:
www.avatarsearch.com
www.sacredsource.com
www.witchvox.com

BIBLIOGRAPHY

Many of the following titles were research material for this book. Some of those referenced will provide a greater understanding of magic in general, some are for explaining the uses of essential oils and herbs, and others are for a better understanding of the cosmology of the ancient Egyptians.

Barrett, Clive. *The Egyptian Gods and Goddesses: The Mythology and Beliefs of Ancient Egypt.* London, UK: Diamond Books, 1996.

Beyerl, Paul. *A Compendium of Herbal Magick.* Blaine, WA: Phoenix Publishing, 1998.

Cunningham, Scott. *The Complete Book of Incense, (and Brews.* St. Paul, MN: Llewellyn Publications,

Dillaire, Claudia R. *Egyptian Love Spells and Rituals.* London, UK: Quantum, 2005.

———. *Egyptian Revenge Spells: Ancient Rituals for Modern Payback.* Berkeley, CA: Ten Speed Press, 2009.

Draco, Melusine. *The Egyptian Book of Days.* Carmarthen, UK: Ignotus Press, 2001.

Eilers, Dana D. *The Practical Pagan.* Franklin Lakes, NJ: New Page Books, 2002.

———. *Pagans and the Law: Understand Your Rights.* Franklin Lakes, NJ: New Page Books, 2003.

Farrar, Janet and Stuart. *The Witches' God: Lord of the Dance.* Blaine, WA: Phoenix Publishing, 1998.

———. *The Witches' Goddess: The Feminine Principle of Divinity.* Blaine, WA: Phoenix Publishing, 1987.

ʹos de Beler, Aude. *Egyptian Mythology.* London, UK: ʹnge Books, 2004.

ʹrge. *A Dictionary of Egyptian Gods and God-* ʹdon, UK: Routledge, 1986.

Holland's Grimoire of Magickal Cor- ʹtual Handbook.* Franklin Lakes, NJ: ʹ6.

ʹils ʹ997.

Houston, Jean. *The Passion of Isis and Osiris: A Gateway to Transcendent Love.* New York: Ballantine Publishing Group, 1995.

Jordan, Michael. *Encyclopedia of Gods: Over 2,500 Deities of the World.* New York: Facts on File, 1993.

Lawless, Julia. *The Complete Illustrated Guide to Aromatherapy: A Practical Approach to the Use of Essential Oils for Health and Well-Being.* London, UK: Element, 2002.

Lurker, Manfred. *An Illustrated Dictionary of the Gods and Symbols of Ancient Egypt.* New York: Thames and Hudson, 1996.

Mercatante, Anthony S. *Who's Who in Egyptian Mythology,* 2nd ed. New York, NY: MetroBooks, 2002.

Morgan, Diane. *The Charmed Garden.* Forres, Scotland, UK: Findhorn Press, 2004.

Morgan, Michele. *Simple Wicca.* Berkeley, CA: Conari Press, 2003.

Redford, Donald B., ed. *The Oxford Essential Guide to Egyptian Mythology.* New York: Berkley Books, 2003.

Rosean, Lexa. *The Encyclopedia of Magickal Ingredients: A Wiccan Guide to Spellcasting*. New Yor: Paraview Pocket Books, 2005.

Smith, Steven R. *Wylundt's Book of Incense: A Magical Primer*. York Beach, ME: Samuel Weiser, 1996.

Webster, Richard. *Write Your Own Magic*. St. Paul, MN: Llewellyn Publications, 2001.

Wildwood, Chrissie. *The Encyclopedia of Aromatherapy*. Rochester, VT: Healing Arts Press, 1996.

Wilkinson, Richard H. *The Complete Gods and Goddesses of Ancient Egypt*. London, UK: Thames and Hudson, 2003.

Yronwode, Catherine. *Hoodoo Herb and Root Magic: A Materia Magica of African-American Conjure*. Forestville, CA: The Lucky Mojo Curio Company, 2002.

INDEX